LAW™

Personal Legal Sourcebooks

• • • • • • • • • • • • •

Contracts

• • • • • • • • • • • • •

MACMILLAN SPECTRUM

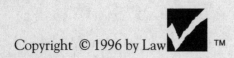
Library of Congress Card Catalog Number: 96-068546
International Standard Book Number: 0-02-861401-1

98 97 96   9 8 7 6 5 4 3 2 1

Interpretation of the printing code: the rightmost number of the first series of numbers is the year of the book's printing; the rightmost number of the second series of numbers is the number of the book's printing. For example, a printing code of 96-1 shows that the first printing occurred in 1996.

Printed in the United States of America

Note: Reasonable care has been taken in the preparation of the text to ensure its clarity and accuracy. This book is sold with the understanding that the author and the publisher are not engaged in rendering legal, accounting, or other professional service. Laws vary from state to state, and readers with specific financial questions should seek the services of a professional advisor.

The author and publisher specifically disclaim any liability, loss or risk, personal or otherwise, which is incurred as a consequence, directly or indirectly, of the use and application of any of the contents of this book.

Book Design by A&D Howell.

Contents

Preface

Welcome to the layman's guide to contracts. The purpose of this book is to provide the general public some information about contracts. It is a reference manual which should answer basic questions. The questions recited in this manual are the more commonly asked questions of attorneys when a client first makes contact for the purpose of entering into a contract. Neither this manual nor the subject matter contained within this manual are in any way a substitute for legal advice. For legal advice, an attorney must be consulted.

The design of this manual is elementary and is, by no means, a comprehensive assessment of a particular legal discipline. It will, however, allow the reader to better understand the various aspects of contract law.

Hopefully, the use of this manual will lessen the personal agony of attempting to look up the answers to the questions covered in the manual. Additionally, the manual should reduce the amount of time the reader will ultimately spend with chosen legal counsel and, therefore, reduce to some degree the costs of legal services.

On the other hand, the manual is also designed to bring to the legal community a better educated public. The massive amount of legal information which is available to the individual attorney would, without question, overwhelm a member of the public who is not trained to research and retrieve the information which would typically apply to a given subject such as contracts. A competent attorney who is skilled in providing legal advice relative to contract law should welcome to his or her office someone with a basic understanding of how contracts are formed. Therefore, the reader should feel comfortable in the fact that through the choice of this manual, it will be possible to meet in the attorney's office with a greater understanding of the subject matter involved.

This manual gives an overview and basic understanding through a question and answer format. It also furnishes some basic forms which most likely would be used in a given state. This manual should provide the general types of forms which an attorney might employ in preparing some of the more basic contracts.

It is never recommended that an individual undertake his or her own representation in such matters as contracts, even though most states do permit such activity. Any individual who is serious about entering into a contract would want to have capable legal assistance and, in that regard, the reader is urged to contact a competent attorney who, as mentioned above, should welcome the fact that a client is arriving at his or her office with the information acquired from this manual. In other words, the reader should be a better informed member of the public by reading and reviewing the contents of this manual and, accordingly, should be better prepared to consult an attorney about using a contract.

Read on, and enjoy the world of contracts!

Introduction

Nearly every American who is not an attorney has, at one time or another, wondered about the legal profession and what it would be like to acquire at least a portion of the knowledge seemingly guarded by the legal community. Many times the average individual has the misconception that attorneys safeguard this information for their own benefit and for the sole purpose of protecting their livelihood. That is not the reason the legal information has not been disseminated to the public. Frankly, no one has undertaken the effort until this time to prepare a system of manuals that would introduce the public to some of the basic information on individual subject areas of the law.

It is not a conspiracy by the legal community to keep information from the general public. It is not because of the unique legal training received by attorneys that information is not readily available to the public. It is not because of the special features of legal language that the information about the law is not found in general reference. The bottom line is simply that there is so very much information written in each state about the laws of that state. In addition, federal laws often apply, and the federal ramifications must be taken into consideration. Consequently, the body of law that relates to a given area or, as we call it in this publication, "discipline" of the law is so immense that even the most skilled attorney in a particular field, such as contract law, would have no way of memorizing or remembering all of the applicable law for that field of study in a single state. The training that an individual attorney receives allows him or her to readily find the necessary material and properly and skillfully represent the client. Of course, we're speaking of competent attorneys, and the public should understand that the majority of attorneys fall into that category.

The vast body of law that is available to attorneys is often available to the general public either through a public library in some instances or through a law library generally situated at a law school, a major university, or a major corporation. Many times the librarians of those facilities will permit members of the public to browse through the legal information that is also available to attorneys. However, without appropriate training, those attempting to ascertain answers to even simple questions may find themselves spending endless hours or days on a particular subject. They may also end up misleading themselves if they allow their research to take them in a wrong direction. Therefore, despite what many people believe, there is a vital need for the legal community and competent legal advice. On the other hand, there is an equally vital need for the public to have access to understandable legal reference material in order to be better informed when contacting their attorney.

The LAW™ Manual and Presentation

Since there has been so much confusion regarding any particular subject area of the law, and since that confusion seems to increase due to the limited reporting of various legal matters by the media, an eminent need exists for the general public to have at their fingertips some basic information about the law and particular legal subjects. In an effort to bring the general public up to speed, Lawchek undertook the publication of various manuals on various topics of the law in order to bring some of the basic information to the general public in readable form. In turn, it is the expectation of Lawchek that the public will be better informed when conferring with a member of the legal community on a given subject of the law. The Lawchek philosophy is to break the legal material down by subject matter.

Throughout the publications provided by Lawchek, the consumer will observe that even though the general topics are broken down by state, there are numerous instances where federal law might be significant and apply to a given question. In those cases, a synopsis of the federal law has been provided so that members of the public can, in turn, inquire of their legal counsel appropriately. The general public also needed to be guided through a system by which the topics of general concern could be identified and explained. Consequently, Lawchek divided the subject matter not only by state but by discipline.

Disciplines of the Law

The disciplines, or topics of the law, that have been chosen by Lawchek are the disciplines that Lawchek surveys indicate to be matters of most common interest. There are literally thousands of topics for research under the general body of law, and hundreds of those topics break down even further into subtopics. Many of the topics and subtopics can be interrelated and essentially cross the paths of other topics depending upon a factual scenario that may develop in a given situation. For example, a corporation may have a contract with an individual and that contract, in turn, may be involved with financing through a particular bank that, in turn, may require certain collateral and a specific form of insurance. In this scenario, it is understandable that corporation law, contract law, the uniform commercial code, banking law, and insurance law might all apply, to name the most obvious. In a more specific area from the same scenario, it might be necessary for an appropriate application of a secured transaction to fall under the uniform commercial code and, in such cases, a particular form for filing with either a secretary of state or the local county recorder may come into the picture. It can be seen from this simple example that the various topics or disciplines of the law are so interrelated that an effort by your attorney to research the particulars under any one of those topics may be necessary.

It is not the purpose of the Lawchek information or reference manual, which you now have in your hand, to deal with any in-depth legal issues that would obviously involve the research of a competent attorney. This manual is exclusively designed to enable you to have an overview of the discipline (in this case, contracts) before you consult with your attorney and/or before you decide whether you do or do not feel you should enter that contract. The structure by Lawchek into the discipline method of reference explanations for the public is also provided to give the public an appreciation of the type of format that is used in presenting a legal document. An example of this would be an apartment lease, which may be presented to both parties for signing. By having an awareness of the forms as well as an awareness of the basic information about the discipline, you should be far better equipped to consult your attorney about contracts.

Lawchek has identified thirty disciplines that either are now available or will soon be available through either Macmillan General Reference or Macmillan Library Reference.

- Administrative Law
- Agricultural Law
- Banking
- Bankruptcy
- Business/Commercial Law
- Contracts
- Criminal
- Corporations
- Domestic/Family Law
- Education
- Eminent Domain/Condemnation
- Elderly
- Environment
- Estates and Wills
- Health
- Insurance

- Intellectual Property (Patent/Copyright)
- International Law (Nafta/Trade)
- Interstate Commerce
- Investments/Brokerage
- Landlord/Tenant
- Manufacturing
- Media (TV-Common Radio, Newspaper)
- Partnerships
- Real Estate
- Social Security
- Sports Law
- Taxation
- Transportation
- Trials/Litigation
- Truth in Lending

Is a Little Knowledge Dangerous?

There is no doubt that a little knowledge in the wrong hands may be dangerous, especially if that knowledge is misused or misinterpreted. That is why Lawchek recommends that the reader contact a competent attorney before entering a contract. Presently, the public has far too little knowledge at its fingertips about the law and the legal community. This lack of knowledge has created many misconceptions about contract law. The design and purpose of this manual is to increase your knowledge and bring you to a better understanding of the subject matter of contracts.

The information contained in this manual is basic, practical information. The manual is designed to bring to you some knowledge about the subject matter of contracts. Lawchek wants the general public to be better informed about the law and recognizes, as Lawchek is certain the reader does, that if you're going to do something, do it right. This manual is designed to take you to that first step so that you have a basic understanding of contracts before you confer with an attorney. This will enable you to make a better choice as to which attorney you might select to represent you in forming a contract. This manual will place you in a better position when it comes to understanding the legal work involved in entering into a contract. Remember, you do want your contract to be stated properly and you want to have an understanding of what is being done. This manual will help you with a better understanding of legal processes. Selecting a competent attorney who understands contracts is part of doing it right.

How to Use This Book

This book is divided into five sections:

Chapter 1—Definition of Terms. Various terms used throughout this book are defined in Chapter 1. These definitions will assist you with the legal language used throughout and give you a better idea about contracts in general.

Chapter 2—Do's and Don'ts. Chapter 2 deals with major pitfalls that can occur and the fact that there are certain things you will want to do and certain things you will not want to do in entering into a contract. At any time where there is doubt, you should consult your attorney.

Chapter 3—Questions and Answers. A question and answer format is set forth in Chapter 3. These are the questions most commonly asked about contracts. The answers to these questions may relate specifically to your state.

Chapter 4—Sample Forms. Generally, the forms are tailored for a particular state. In this manual, they are generic and must be modified for particular state use. These forms are current to the date of this publication. If legislative enactments have occurred since the publication date, the forms may need to be changed accordingly. This is why it is important to consult your attorney.

Chapter 5—Blank Forms. The forms in this chapter are blank versions of the completed forms in Chapter 4; these forms are for your use.

The recommended practice for the use of this manual is for you to find the question that concerns you in the question and answer portion, then find the form that applies in the form section. We recommend that you first read the section on common terms. By cross-referencing between the questions and answers and the appropriate forms, you will see that it is much easier to understand the forms and much easier to prepare them for your attorney.

Because the information provided by Lawchek may not be all-inclusive to contract law, you are advised that any questions you have that go beyond the questions and answers or forms provided in this manual should be presented to your attorney. Although the material contained in all of Lawchek's manuals has been written by attorneys, these attorneys are located throughout the United States and focus their study of law in particular areas. It would both be improper and unethical for Lawchek to serve as a clearinghouse in referring you to those attorneys. Therefore, Lawchek cannot and will not make such references but encourages you to contact your own attorney with skills in the area of contracts. Should you need assistance in locating such an attorney, you should contact the Bar Association for a listing of names of attorneys in your state who do practice in the area of contract law.

Codes, Sections, and Subsections

Throughout the Lawchek program, references are made to legal codes, sections, and subsections (§). Some examples of these references follow: Massachusetts Code 23185P; Section 3109.01 of the Ohio Revised Code; §4-27-301 of the Arkansas Code. Should you choose to research this legal information on your own, the information may be accessed at the law library of a major college or university. However, it should be noted that law libraries are not organized in the same manner as other libraries. Anyone attempting to undertake his or her own research should be prepared to confront a difficult, tedious task. It is very advisable that an attorney or someone else familiar with legal research be consulted.

Acknowledgments

Many people contributed in various ways toward making this legal reference material available to the general public, and it would be impossible to acknowledge them all. However, special thanks must be given to several people who were indispensable to the completion of this booklet.

For his countless hours of legal research and his ability to convert that research into text that is understandable to those not having a legal background, Lawchek would like to thank Attorney Richard A. Pundt.

Lawchek is indebted to Debra A. Shiley and Bette Tropek Miller for their time and diligence in transcribing, proofreading, and editing the booklet and assuring the quality of the final product.

Trademarks and Copyrights

All material of Lawchek is protected with appropriate trademarks and copyrights. Additionally, terms mentioned in this book that are known to be or suspected to be the trademarks or service marks of other companies are capitalized, and such terms and conditions are also capitalized or highlighted or specially acknowledged in the software that may accompany this manual. Lawchek cannot attest to the accuracy of this information. The use of a term in this book should not be regarded as affecting the validity of any trademark or service mark.

CHAPTER • 1

Definition of Terms

Abatement—A reduction, a decrease, or a diminution. The suspension or cessation, in whole or in part, of a continuing charge, such as rent.

Agreement—A meeting of two or more minds; a coming together in opinion or determination; the coming together in accord of two minds on a given proposition.

In law, a concord of understanding and intention between two or more parties with respect to the effect upon their relative rights and duties, of certain past or future facts or performances. The consent of two or more persons concurring respecting the transmission of some property, right, or benefits, with a view of contracting an obligation, a mutual obligation. From *Black's Law Dictionary*, 1990 edition.

A manifestation of mutual assent on the part of two or more persons as to the substance of a contract. *Restatement of Contracts*, Second, of Section 3, etc.

The act of two or more persons, who unite in expressing a mutual and common purpose, with the view of altering their rights and obligations. The union of two or more minds in a thing done or to be done; the mutual assent to do a thing. A compact between parties who are thereby subjected to the obligation or to whom the contemplated right is thereby secured.

Although often used as synonymous with "contract," agreement is a broader term; e.g., an agreement might lack an essential element of a contract. The bargain of the parties in fact as found in their language or by implication from other circumstances including course of dealing or use of trade or course of performance.

Bailment—A delivery of goods or personal property, by one person (bailor) to another (bailee), in trust for the execution of a special object upon or in relation to such goods, beneficial either to the bailor or bailee or both, and upon a contract, expressed or implied, to perform the trust and carry out such object, and thereupon either to redeliver the goods to the bailor or otherwise dispose of the same in conformity with the purpose of the trust. From *Black's Law Dictionary*, 1990 edition.

Bilateral contract—A bilateral contract is also known as a reciprocal contract and is defined as a contract by which the parties expressly enter into mutual engagements such as a sale or hire. From *Black's Law Dictionary*, 1990 edition.

Breach of contract—Failure, without legal excuse, to perform any promise which forms the whole or part of a contract. Prevention or hindrance by a party to contract of any occurrence or performance requisite under the contract for the creation or continuance of a right in favor of the other party or the discharge of a duty by him. Unequivocal, distinct and absolute refusal to perform agreement. From *Black's Law Dictionary*, 1990 edition.

Conditional contract—A contract whose very existence and performance depends upon the happening of some contingency or condition expressly stated therein. From *Black's Law Dictionary*, 1990 edition.

Consideration—The inducement to a contract. The cause, motive, price, or impelling influence which induces a contracting party to enter into a contract. The reason or material cause of a contract. Some right, interest, profit, or benefit accruing to one party, or some forbearance, detriment, loss, or responsibility, given, suffered, or undertaken by the other. *Restatement of Contracts*, Second, Section 17(1), 71. From *Black's Law Dictionary*, sixth edition.

Consignment—The act or process of consigning goods; the transportation of goods consigned; an article or collection of goods sent to a factor; goods or property sent, by the aid of a common carrier, from one person and one place to another person and another place; something consigned and shipped. Entrusting of goods to another to sell for the consignor. A bailment for sale.

Contract—An agreement between two or more persons which creates an obligation to do or not to do a particular thing. As defined in Restatement, Second, Contracts, Section 3: "A contract is a promise or a set of promises for the breach of which the law gives a remedy, or the performance of which the law in some way recognizes as a duty." From *Black's Law Dictionary*, 1990 edition.

Deed—A conveyance of realty; a writing signed by grantor, whereby title to realty is transferred from one to another. From *Black's Law Dictionary*, 1990 edition.

Dispute— A conflict or controversy; a conflict of claims or rights; an assertion of a right, claim, or demand on one side, met by contrary claims or allegations. From *Black's Law Dictionary*, 1990 edition.

Document—An instrument on which is recorded by means of letters, figures, or marks, the original, official, or legal form of something which may be eventually used. From *Black's Law Dictionary*, 1990 edition.

Earnest money—A sum of money paid by a buyer at the time of entering a contract to indicate the intention and ability of the buyer to carry out the contract.

Normally, earnest money is applied against the purchase price. Often, the contract provides for forfeiture of this sum if the buyer defaults. From *Black's Law Dictionary*, 1990 edition.

Earnings—Income. That which is earned; i.e., money earned from performance of labor, services, sale of goods, etc. Revenue earned by an individual or business. Earnings generally include but are not limited to: salaries and wages, interest and dividends, and income from self-employment. From *Black's Law Dictionary*, 1990 edition.

Emancipation—The act by which one who was unfree, or under the power and control of another, is rendered free, or set at liberty and made his own master. From *Black's Law Dictionary*, 1990 edition.

Employment—An act of employing or state of being employed; that which engages or occupies; that which consumes time or attention; also an occupation, profession, trade, post or business. From *Black's Law Dictionary*, 1990 edition.

Employment contract—An agreement or contract between employer and employee in which the terms or conditions of one's employment are provided. From *Black's Law Dictionary*, 1990 edition.

Escrow—A legal document (such as a deed), money, stock, or other property delivered by the grantor, promissor, or obligator to the hands of a third person to be held by the latter until the happening of a contingency or performance of a condition, and then by him delivered to the grantee, promissee or obligee. From *Black's Law Dictionary*, 1990 edition.

Exculpatory—Clearing or tending to clear from alleged fault or guilt; excusing.

Express contract—An express contract is an actual agreement of the parties, the terms of which are openly uttered or declared at the time of making it, being stated in distinct and explicit language, either orally or in writing. From *Black's Law Dictionary*, 1990 edition.

Implied contract—An implied contract is one not created or evidenced by the explicit agreement of the parties, but inferred by the law as a matter of reason and justice from their acts or conduct, circumstances surrounding the transaction making it a reasonable, or even a necessary, assumption that a contract existed between them by tacit understanding. From *Black's Law Dictionary*, 1990 edition.

Independent contractor—Generally, one who, in exercise of an independent employment, contracts to do a piece of work according to his own methods and is subject to his employer's control only as to end product or final result of his work. From *Black's Law Dictionary*, 1990 edition.

Infancy (minority)—Infancy or minority is the state of a person who is under the age of legal majority—at common law, twenty-one years; now, generally, eighteen years. According to the sense in which this term is used, it may denote the condition of the person with reference to his years, or the contractual disabilities which non-age initials, or his status with regard to other powers or relation.

At common law, children under the age of seven are conclusively presumed to be without criminal capacity; those who have reached the age of fourteen are treated as fully responsible, while as to those between the ages of seven and fourteen, there is a rebuttal presumption of criminal incapacity. Many states have made some change by statute in the age of criminal responsibility for minors. In addition, all jurisdictions have adopted juvenile court legislation providing that some or all criminal conduct by those persons under a certain age (usually age eighteen) must or may be adjudicated in the juvenile court rather than in criminal prosecution. See *Black's Law Dictionary*, 1990 edition.

Intent—Design, resolve, or determination with which a person acts. A state of mind in which a person seeks to accomplish a given result through a course of action. From *Black's Law Dictionary*, 1990 edition.

Inure—To take effect; to result. In property law, to come to the benefit of a person or to fix his interest therein.

Investment contract—A contract in which one party invests money or property expecting return on his investment. From *Black's Law Dictionary*, 1990 edition.

Joint and several—A joint contract is one made by two or more promissors, who are jointly bound to fulfill its obligations, or made to two or more promissees, who are jointly entitled to require performance of the same. A contract may be "several" as to any one of several promissors or promissees, if a person has a legal right (either from the terms of the agreement or the nature of the undertaking) to enforce his individual interest separately from the other parties. Generally, all contracts are joint where the interest of the parties benefitting from the contract is joint, and separate where that interest is separate. *Black's Law Dictionary*, 1990 edition.

Lease—Any agreement which gives rise to relationship of landlord and tenant (real property) or lessor and lessee (real or personal property). A contract for exclusive possession of lands, tenements or hereditaments for life, for term of years, at will, or for any interest less than that of lessor, usually for a specified rent or compensation. From *Black's Law Dictionary*, 1990 edition.

Majority—Full age; legal age; the age at which, by law, a person is entitled to the management of his own affairs and to the enjoyment of civic rights.

Mortgage—Mortgage is an interest in land created by a written instrument providing security for the performance of a duty or payment of a debt. From *Black's Law Dictionary*, 1990 edition.

Mutual promise—Promises simultaneously made by and between two parties; each promise being the consideration for the other. From *Black's Law Dictionary*, 1990 edition.

Note—An instrument containing an express and absolute promise of signer (i.e., maker) to pay to a specified person or order, or bearer, a definite sum of money at a specified time. An instrument that is a promise to pay, other than a certificate of deposit. UCC Section 3-104(2)(d). Two party instrument made by the maker and payable to payee which is negotiable as signed by the maker and contains an unconditional promise to pay sum certain in money, on demand or at a definite time, to order or bearer. UCC Section 3-104(1). A note not meeting these requirements may be assignable but not negotiable. See *Black's Law Dictionary*, 1990 edition.

There are several notes including: a collateral note, which is a two party instrument containing a promise to pay and secure by pledge of property such as security, real estate, etc.; a demand note which is a note payable on demand as contrasted with a time note which is payable at a definite time in the future; an installment note which is one of a series of notes payable at regular intervals; a single note calling for payment and installments at fixed periods of time; a joint and several note, which is a note signed by persons as makers who agree to be bound, jointly and severally; i.e., they may be joined in a suit or they may be sued separately; joint note which is a note evidencing indebtedness with two or more persons agreeing to be liable jointly and for payment of which all such persons may be joined in an action to recover; mortgage note which is a note evidencing a loan for which real estate has been offered as security; a negotiable note which is a note signed by the maker, containing an unconditional promise to pay a certain sum in money which is payable on demand or at a definite time to order or bearer; and secured note which is a note for which security in the form of either real or personal property has been pledged or mortgaged. See Uniform Commercial Code Section 3-104(1).

Obligation—A generic word, derived from a Latin substantive "obligatio," having many, wide, and varied meanings according to the context in which it is used. That which a person is bound to do or forebear; any duty imposed by law, promise, contract, relations of society, courtesy, kindness, etc. From *Black's Law Dictionary*, 1990 edition.

Obligor—A promissor. The person who has engaged to perform some obligation. Person obligated under a contract or bond.

Offset—A deduction; a counterclaim; a contrary claim or demand by which a given claim may be lessened or canceled. An "offset" may be defined as a claim that serves to counterbalance or to compensate for another claim.

Open end contract—Contract (normally sales contract) in which certain terms (e.g. order amount) are deliberately left open. From *Black's Law Dictionary*, 1990 edition.

Parental consent—Consent required of minor from parent to marry or to take other legal obligations. From *Black's Law Dictionary*, 1990 edition.

Parol contract—An oral contract as distinguished from a written or formal contract.

Performance—The fulfillment or accomplishment of a promise, contract, or other obligation, according to its terms, relieving such person of all further obligation or liability thereunder. From *Black's Law Dictionary*, 1990 edition.

Personal contract—A contract relating to personal property, or one which so far involves the element of personal knowledge or skill or personal confidence that it can be performed only by the person with whom made, and therefore is not binding on his executor. From *Black's Law Dictionary*, 1990 edition.

Promise—A declaration which binds the person who makes it, either in honor, conscience, or law, to do or forbear a certain, specific act, and which gives to the person to whom made a right to expect or claim the performance of some particular thing. From *Black's Law Dictionary*, 1990 edition.

Purchase—Transmission of property from one person to another by a voluntary act and agreement, founded on valuable consideration. To own by paying or by promising to pay an agreed price which is enforceable at law. From *Black's Law Dictionary*, 1990 edition.

Quasi contract—Legal fiction invented by common law courts to permit recovery by contractual remedy in cases where, in fact, there is no contract, but where circumstances are such that justice warrants a recovery as though there had been a promise. From *Black's Law Dictionary*, 1990 edition.

Special contract—A contract under seal; a specialty; as distinguished from one merely oral or in writing not sealed. From *Black's Law Dictionary*, 1990 edition.

Subcontract—A contract subordinate to another contract, made or intended to be made between the contracting parties, on the one part, or some of them, and a third party (i.e. subcontractor). From *Black's Law Dictionary*, 1990 edition.

Unconscionable contract—A contract which no sensible man not under delusion, duress, or in distress would make, and such as no honest and fair man would accept. From *Black's Law Dictionary*, 1990 edition.

Unenforceable contract—An unenforceable contract is one for the breach of which neither the remedy of damages nor the remedy of specific performance is available, but which is recognized in some other way as creating a duty of performance, though there has been no ratification. *Restatement of Contracts*, Second, Section 8. When a contract has some legal consequences that may not be enforced in an action for damages or specific performance in the face of certain defenses, such as the statute of fraud or the statute of limitations, the contract is said to be "unenforceable."

Unilateral contract—A unilateral contract is one in which one party makes an express engagement or undertakes a performance without receiving in return any express engagement or promise of performance from the other. From *Black's Law Dictionary*, 1990 edition.

Written contract—A written contract is one in which all of its terms are in writing. It is commonly referred to as a formal contract. From *Black's Law Dictionary*, 1990 edition.

CHAPTER 2

Do's and Don'ts

Do

Read this manual.

Remember to consult an attorney for legal problems.

Read the questions and answers in order to have a basic understanding of the subject matter that you have chosen, in this case, contracts.

Pay special attention to detail, especially when completing forms for your attorney.

Approach contracting as a serious matter that requires patience for the long term and guidance to complete.

Enjoy the materials presented and use the materials for your benefit in acquiring new knowledge.

Don't

Make assumptions about contract law.

Expect this manual to be the substitute or a replacement for an attorney's implementation of drafting a contract.

Expect that the questions and answers embellish all aspects of a contract.

Expect the forms contained here to be the only forms that you may need.

Rush through the materials or make assumptions (consult an attorney).

Expect that just anyone will have the answers to your questions. Read the manual and talk to your attorney.

Questions and Answers

What is a contract?

Generally, a contract is understood to be an agreement that creates an obligation upon one party. Its basic components include (1) parties who are capable of contracting, (2) a particular subject matter, (3) legal consideration or monetary value, (4) a common ground of agreement, and (5) an obligation that is mutual between the parties.

A contract is an expression by two or more persons of common intention to effect their legal relations.

What is consideration?

Consideration for a contract is the inducement from one party to another to form the contract. The cause, motive, price, or impelling influence that induces a contracting party to enter into a contract is generally underlying consideration. (See *Black's Law Dictionary*, 1990 edition.) Consideration generally is some right, interest, profit, or benefit accruing to one party, or some forbearance, detriment, loss, or responsibility that is given, suffered, or undertaken by the other. (See *Restatement of Contracts*, Second, Sections 17(1), 17.)

Consideration is frequently defined as "a benefit to the party promising or a loss or detriment to the party to whom the promise is made."

What is the content of a contract?

In establishing a basic contract, attention should be given to: (1) proper identification of the parties; (2) the date of the contract; (3) the term or period of time over which the contract should apply; (4) the purpose of the contract; (5) the amount of consideration, compensation payment, or cost; (6) the duties or obligations of the parties; (7) the specific item, property, location, territory, or consequence to which the contract applies; (8) liability or insurance coverage relative to possible loss; (9) conditions under which the contract may be terminated; (10) changes or modifications to the contract terms; (11) special restrictions such as covenants not to compete; (12) maintenance, repairs, additions, or modifications to a product used; (13) provisions relating to an assignment of the contract; (14) conditions under which portions of the contract may be waived; (15) interest on unpaid amounts; (16) renewal options; (17) special provisions or the application of special rules, laws, regulations, etc.; and (18) the state laws to which the contract may apply. The foregoing are some examples of the type of provisions that may need to be included in a typical contract. An attorney will be able to discuss each of these items and others with you.

What is an express contract?

An express contract is a contract where the intention of the parties and the terms and conditions of the agreement are declared or "expressed" by the parties, at the time the parties form the contract. An express contract may be made either in writing or orally. It is possible for a third party to consummate the contract, such as in a real estate transaction, when certain conditions are dependent upon the happening of another event.

In an express contract, the parties specifically have declared the terms and conditions. This has been done either orally or in writing at the time the contract has been made. Generally, such contracts are in two categories, one being under seal such as specialty, and the other by parol. A parol contract is an oral contract as distinguished from a written or formal contract.

What is an implied contract?

An implied contract is frequently understood to be a contract of two classes. The first implied contract is a contract implied in fact, and the second is a contract implied in law.

An implied contract is one not created or evidenced by the exclusive agreement of the parties. An implied contract is inferred by the law, as a matter of reason and justice from the acts or conduct of the involved parties. The circumstances surrounding the transaction make it reasonable, or even a necessary assumption that a contract existed between them by tacit understanding. (From *Black's Law Dictionary*, 1990 edition.)

What is an oral contract?

An oral contract is usually something verbal between parties. The oral contract may, and usually does, consist of a mere conversation that may be specific as to the intent of the parties, or it may be a general consensus or agreement. An oral contract can actually be created without the spoken word. Even though an oral contract may not involve a written document, written evidence may be introduced in order to establish the contractual relationship or to substantiate the position of the parties. Written documentation evidencing the prior oral agreement or contract does not make the contract a written contract unless the specific memorandum, letter, or other written document is mutually adopted by the parties.

An oral contract has a legally binding effect under the law so long as the elements of contracts such as a promise, consideration (a monetary matter), an agreement to act, or a forbearance are parts of the agreement. Such agreement must have been reached by consenting individuals who had the capacity to legally obligate themselves.

The fact that a contract is oral does not minimize the fact that it is a legal relationship consisting of the rights and duties of the contracting parties. With basic elements such as legal consideration, mutuality of agreement, and mutuality of obligation, a contract may be reached orally.

What is a written contract?

A written contract is generally a contract in legible format, such as written characters and numbers. It is a contract in which all of the terms are in writing, and the writing must be legible. Generally, it is understood that a written memorandum is not identical to the written contract but is only evidence of it and usually does not contain all the terms of a written contract. A written agreement, however, does not lose its force as a written contract because parol evidence or oral statements are necessary to explain some of the terms.

A contract that is not entirely in writing is regarded as an oral or verbal contract. An agreement may be oral, although there is a written note of memorandum substantiating the terms of the oral agreement. Oral statements or parol evidence may be used to clarify a written contract; nevertheless, a written contract is generally a contract which is set forth in some form of legible characters such as writing.

What is a standard contract?

A contract may and should be written for the specific interests, needs, requirements, and agreements between the contracting parties. However, often standardized forms of contracts are developed for repeated and common usage when specific purposes are intended. For example, the state bar association may develop and disseminate for use standardized contracts for real estate transactions, farm lease agreements, rental agreements, and certain security agreements, to name a few. Banks and banking associations have developed standardized contract forms for security agreements, notes, and mortgages. Regulatory agencies and real estate firms have developed forms for the purchase and sale of property, along with certain escrow contract form sheets. Medical societies, hospitals, and doctors' offices have developed certain consent forms, waiver forms, and contracts for admission and payment purposes. Retailers have developed forms for credit purchases, repayment plans, and layaway programs. Contractors often use standardized contracts for home purchases, change orders, and lien waivers. Insurance companies have developed many uniform contracts that relate to the purchase of liability insurance, health insurance, life insurance, etc. Such contracts are often called adhesion contracts.

What is an adhesion contract?

An adhesion contract is a standardized contract form offered to consumers for goods and services on essentially a take-it-or-leave-it basis. A typical example of an adhesion contract is an insurance policy. The adhesion contract rarely affords the consumer any realistic opportunity to bargain for special provisions under the contract. The conditions of the adhesion contract are generally such that the consumer cannot obtain a desired product or service unless the consumer acquiesces in the form of a contract that is presented. A distinctive feature of the adhesion contract is that the weaker party has no realistic choice as to its terms. The trend by the courts is to relieve parties from any unfair conditions imposed by the adhesion contract since the court recognizes that these adhesion contracts are not the result of a traditionally bargained position.

What is a unilateral contract?

A unilateral contract is one in which one party makes an express engagement or undertakes a performance without receiving in return any express engagement or promise of performance from the other. (From *Black's Law Dictionary*.)

What is a quasi contract?

According to *Black's Law Dictionary*, a quasi contract is a legal fiction invented by common law courts to permit the recovery by a contractual remedy in cases where, in fact, there is no contract, but where circumstances are such that justice warrants a recovery as though there had been a promise. It is not based upon intention or consent of the parties but is founded on considerations of justice and equity and on the doctrine of unjust enrichment. It is not, in fact, a contract, but an obligation that the law creates in absence of any agreement. It occurs when and because the acts of the parties or others have placed in the possession of one person money or its equivalent, under such circumstances that, in equity and good conscience, he should not retain. It is what was formally known as the contract implied in law. It has no reference to the intentions or expressions of the parties.

What is an illegal contract?

An illegal contract exists where the formation of the contract or the performance of the contract is expressly forbidden by the state's statutes or by federal statutes. The statute may either be civil or criminal in nature and occurs where a penalty is imposed by law for the execution or completion of some act that is determined by state law to be against public policy and, therefore, illegal.

What is a lease?

A lease is any agreement that gives rise to a relationship of landlord and tenant (real property) or lessor and lessee (real or personal property). It is a contract for exclusive possession of lands, tenements, or hereditaments for life, for term or years, at will, or for any interest less than that of lessor, usually for a specified rent or compensation. (From *Black's Law Dictionary*, 1990 edition.)

What is a legal purpose?

Contracts may be established for any legal purpose. A variety of reasons may exist for a contract; however, regardless of the purpose of the contract, it must be legal in the state. The different types of commonly used contracts include, but are not limited to, loans, promissory notes, mortgages, real estate purchase agreements, stocks, bonds, security agreements, employment contracts, construction contracts, usage contracts (such as land easements, land rental, vehicle rental, machine rental, software license, name license), and various forms of leases. A contract may not be written for any purpose that is contrary to either state or federal laws. For example, a contract may not be written in such a manner that requires either party to perform a criminal act or engage in activity that would be a violation of the law. A contract may not be written that would allow for a usurious rate of interest. A contract may not be written that requires a party to meet a deadline over the roadways that would require a party to travel at rates of speed in excess of the posted speed limits.

What is breach or default?

A breach is a failure or omission of performing something that should be done, usually as specified by contract. It is usually an omission or failure to perform a legal or contractual duty. Oftentimes, it is the failure to observe a promise or to discharge an obligation such as to pay interest or principal on a debt when due.

A breach of contract is the failure to perform a promise without a legal excuse. It is the unequivocal, distinct, and absolute refusal to perform an agreement. It is in sum and substance a failure to perform an obligation.

What is modification?

It is possible for the parties to a contract to modify the terms and conditions of a contract. Any modification to a contract must be done through the consent of the contracting parties. In other words, if there are two parties to a contract, both parties must agree to the modifications or changes to the contract. If there are three parties, then all three parties must agree, etc. Modifications to contracts are common and often result when both parties want the contract to be fulfilled. However, if allowance is not made for a sufficient amount of time for the performance of the contract, or if some other vital provision of the agreement had not been included in the actual contract itself, a modification may occur. Contract modification may result from the direct meetings of the parties or through correspondence between the parties. The item that has been overlooked, which needs to be modified, is brought by one party to the attention of the other party, and both parties agree to the specific terms and conditions of such modifications. Modifications to contracts are generally handled in two ways: (1) either the contract is rewritten to accept the modification; or (2) an addendum is prepared to the contract and signed by the parties, all of whom acknowledge the fact that the addendum should be a part of the main contract and agree further that the addendum modifies the initial contract. The addendum should always relate back to the initial contract between the parties and should specifically state the purposes for which the addendum is modifying the initial contract.

What is a mortgage?

A mortgage is an interest in land created by a written instrument providing security for the performance of a duty or payment of a debt. (From *Black's Law Dictionary*, 1990 edition.)

What is a note?

A note is an instrument containing an express and absolute promise of signer (i.e., maker) to pay to a specified person or order, or bearer, a definite sum of money at a specified rate. An instrument that is a promise to pay, other than a certificate of deposit. (From *Black's Law Dictionary*, 1990 edition.)

What is legal age?

Alabama: An individual may not be considered to reach an age of majority until a specific time under state law; however, a minor may engage in contracting for necessities and/or other items including employment. Once performance is made, payment shall be made either to or by the minor depending upon whether the payment or whether the benefits to the contract are received or given by the minor. A parent cannot collect a second time when payment has been made to a minor for a service such as an employment service when rendered. A minor may, however, repudiate a contract within a reasonable time after reaching majority. In the state of Alabama, the legal age for most purposes is the age of nineteen (19). For particular information relative to legal age in Alabama, see Code Section 26-1-1. Its effective date was July 22, 1975.

Alaska: An individual may not be considered to reach an age of majority until a specific time under state law; however, a minor may engage in contracting for necessities and/or other items including employment. Once performance is made, payment shall be made either to or by the minor depending upon whether the payment or whether the benefits to the contract are received or given by the minor. A parent cannot collect a second time when payment has been made to a minor for a service such as an employment service when rendered. A minor may, however, repudiate a contract within a reasonable time after reaching majority. The legal age in Alaska is the age of eighteen (18). This became effective in 1977. (See Code Section 25.20.010.)

Arizona: Legal age is defined as the age of majority. In the state of Arizona, legal age is eighteen (18) years for both men and women (see Revised Statute Section 1-215). However, in the case of consumption of alcoholic beverages, the legal age is twenty-one (21) years for both men and women. Children may contract for employment in the state of Arizona; however, the employment of children of specific ages may be prohibited in certain circumstances. (See Section 23-230 et. seq. of the Arizona Statutes.)

Arkansas: An individual may not be considered to reach an age of majority until a specific time under state law; however, a minor may engage in contracting for necessities and/or other items including employment. Once performance is made, payment shall be made either to or by the minor depending upon whether the payment or whether the benefits to the contract are received or given by the minor. A parent cannot collect a second time when payment has been made to a minor for a service such as an employment service when rendered. A minor may, however, repudiate a contract within a reasonable time after reaching majority. The legal age in Arkansas is the age of eighteen (18). Drinking is permitted at the age of twenty-one (21). The age of majority is governed under Section 9.25-101. A form of license for marriage is provided for pursuant to Section 9-11-201; however, no marriage license shall be issued to anyone unless the female is at least the age of sixteen (16) and the male is at least the age of seventeen (17). For a male or female under the age of eighteen (18), a marriage license can only be issued with the written consent of the parent or guardian.

California: An individual may not be considered to reach an age of majority until a specific time under state law; however, a minor may engage in contracting for necessities and/or other items including employment. Once performance is made, payment shall be made either to or by the minor depending upon whether the payment or whether the benefits to the contract are received or given by the minor. A parent cannot collect a second time when payment has been made to a minor for a service such as an employment service when rendered. A minor may, however, repudiate a contract within a reasonable time after reaching majority. The recognized legal age in the state of California is eighteen (18) years or older. See the following Family Code Sections: 6500, 6501 and 6502.

Colorado: An individual may not be considered to reach an age of majority until a specific time under state law; however, a minor may engage in contracting for necessities and/or other items including employment. Once performance is made, payment shall be made either to or by the minor depending upon whether the payment or whether the benefits to the contract are received or given by the minor. A parent cannot collect a second time when payment has been made to a minor for a service such as an employment service when rendered. A minor may, however, repudiate a contract within a reasonable time after reaching majority. Legal age in the state of Colorado is eighteen (18) years of age or older. See Code Section 13-22-101 with an effective date of July 1, 1973.

Connecticut: An individual may not be considered to reach an age of majority until a specific time under state law; however, a minor may engage in contracting for necessities and/or other items including employment. Once performance is made, payment shall be made either to or by the minor depending upon whether the payment or whether the benefits to the contract are received or given by the minor. A parent cannot collect a second time when payment has been made to a minor for a service such as an employment service when rendered. A minor may, however, repudiate a contract within a reasonable time after reaching majority. The legal age in the state of Connecticut is eighteen (18) years of age. See Title 1, Section 1-1D. The effective date of this statute was 1972. For general purposes, a person at the age of eighteen (18) may contract in the state of Connecticut.

Delaware: In the state of Delaware, anyone over the age of eighteen (18) is considered to be of legal age and an adult. See Section 1-302 and Section 1-701. Anyone over the age of eighteen (18) may contract freely without consideration of an adult. However, individuals under the age of eighteen (18) may engage in employment contracts under certain circumstances. Parents are responsible for liability up to $5,000 for their children under age eighteen (18) who live with them, in the event of any destruction or damage caused by the child. The person under the age of twenty-one (21) may not buy alcoholic beverages; see Section 4-904.

Florida: An individual may not be considered to reach an age of majority until a specific time under state law; however, a minor may engage in contracting for necessities and/or other items including employment. Once performance is made, payment shall be made either to or by the minor depending upon whether the payment or whether the benefits to the contract are received or given by the minor. A parent cannot collect a second time when payment has been made to a minor for a service such as an employment service when rendered. A minor may, however, repudiate a contract within a reasonable time after reaching majority. In Florida, the legal age is eighteen (18) years of age. An individual's age of majority is covered under Section 743.07, and that is eighteen (18) years of age for purposes such as contracting. For the consumption of alcohol, an individual in the state of Florida must be twenty-one (21) years of age. (See Section 561.15).

Georgia: An individual may not be considered to reach an age of majority until a specific time under state law; however, a minor may engage in contracting for necessities and/or other items including employment. Once performance is made, payment shall be made either to or by the minor depending upon whether the payment or whether the benefits to the contract are received or given by the minor. A parent cannot collect a second time when payment has been made to a minor for a service such as an employment service when rendered. A minor may, however, repudiate a contract within a reasonable time after reaching majority. The legal age or age of majority in the state of Georgia is eighteen (18) years of age. (See Code Section 74-104.) Each state has its own unique age features and, in Georgia, a person under the age of sixteen (16) may not hunt deer. (See Section 45-518.)

Hawaii: In Hawaii, an individual may not be considered to reach the age of majority until a specific time under state law; however, a minor may engage in contracting for necessities and/or other items including employment. Once performance is made, payment shall be made either to or by the minor depending upon whether the payment or whether the benefits to the contract are received or given by the minor. A parent cannot collect a second time when payment has been made to a minor for a service such as an employment service when rendered. A minor may, however, repudiate a contract within a reasonable time after reaching majority. The legal age for contracting in the state of Hawaii is eighteen (18) years of age. (See Code Section 5577.1.) Hawaii has, as every other state, unique features relative to the regulation of individuals under age. For example, there is a curfew on individuals sixteen (16) years or younger between 10:00 P.M. and 4:00 A.M. (See Section 577.16).

Idaho: An individual may not be considered to reach an age of majority until a specific time under state law; however, a minor may engage in contracting for necessities and/or other items including employment. Once performance is made, payment shall be made either to or by the minor depending upon whether the payment or whether the benefits to the contract are received or given by the minor. A parent cannot collect a second time when payment has been made to a minor for a service such as an employment service when rendered. A minor may, however, repudiate a contract within a reasonable time after reaching majority. The legal age in the state of Idaho is eighteen (18) years of age. (See Code Section 32-101.) No one under the age of nineteen (19) may consume alcoholic beverages. (See proof of age requirement, Section 23-1013.)

Illinois: An individual may not be considered to reach an age of majority until a specific time under state law; however, a minor may engage in contracting for necessities and/or other items including employment. Once performance is made, payment shall be made either to or by the minor, depending upon whether the payment or whether the benefits to the contract are received or given by the minor. A parent cannot collect a second time when payment has been made to a minor for a service such as an employment service when rendered. A minor may, however, repudiate a contract within a reasonable time after reaching majority. The legal age to contract in the state of Illinois is eighteen (18). However, a mature minor, pursuant to 750 ILCS 30/3.2, which provides that a person sixteen (16) or older but under the age of eighteen (18) who has demonstrated an ability to manage his own affairs and to live independently from a parent or guardian, may be considered to be a person of legal age. For additional information relating to legal age in the state of Illinois, see 750 ILCS 30/1 et. seq.

Indiana: An individual may not be considered to reach an age of majority until a specific time under state law; however, a minor may engage in contracting for necessities and/or other items including employment. Once performance is made, payment shall be made either to or by the minor depending upon whether the payment or whether the benefits to the contract are received or given by the minor. A parent cannot collect a second time when payment has been made to a minor for a service such as an employment service when rendered. A minor may, however, repudiate a contract within a reasonable time after reaching majority. The legal age in the state of Indiana is eighteen (18) years for the purpose of contracting. (See Section 34-1-2-5.5.) For consumption of alcoholic beverages, the legal age is twenty-one (21); therefore, it is illegal to sell alcohol to anyone who is a minor or under the age of twenty-one (21) in the state of Indiana. (See Section 7.1-5-7-5.1.)

Iowa: The legal age in the state of Iowa is the age of eighteen (18). The consent of parents or guardians is required for certain contracts or obligations if the individual is under the age of eighteen (18). For example, if an individual wishes to marry under the age of eighteen (18), parental consent is required. (See Section 595.3 of the Code of Iowa.)

In Probate matters, court has the authority to appoint a guardian for an individual who is a minor (an individual under the age of eighteen [18]). See Section 633.556 of the Code of Iowa. A guardian may also be appointed for a person or property of any person other than a minor under fourteen (14), upon that individual's own application. (See Section 633.557.)

In Iowa, an individual obtains his or her majority by virtue of a marriage. Any individual who is convicted as an adult, even though under the age of eighteen (18), is considered to have reached the age of majority. (See Section 599.1 Code of Iowa.)

As to contracts, a minor is bound by his or her contract for life necessities and for any other contract in which an individual under eighteen (18) years of age engages, unless the contract is disaffirmed within a reasonable time after the individual reaches the age of majority or is otherwise emancipated. (See Section 599.2 of the Code of Iowa.)

Kansas: An individual may not be considered to reach an age of majority until a specific time under state law; however, a minor may engage in contracting for necessities and/or other items including employment. Once performance is made, payment shall be made either to or by the minor depending upon whether the payment or whether the benefits to the contract are received or given by the minor. A parent cannot collect a second time when payment has been made to a minor for a service such as an employment service when rendered. A minor may, however, repudiate a contract within a reasonable time after reaching majority. The legal age for contracting and for most other purposes in the state of Kansas is the age of eighteen (18). (See Code Section 38-101.) However, anyone who has obtained the age of sixteen (16) and is married is considered to have obtained the age of majority and is capable of contracting.

Kentucky: An individual may not be considered to reach an age of majority until a specific time under state law; however, a minor may engage in contracting for necessities and/or other items including employment. Once performance is made, payment shall be made either to or by the minor depending upon whether the payment or whether the benefits to the contract are received or given by the minor. A parent cannot collect a second time when payment has been made to a minor for a service such as an employment service when rendered. A minor may, however, repudiate a contract within a reasonable time after reaching majority. The age of majority in the state of Kentucky is eighteen (18) years of age for all purposes except consuming alcohol. For the consumption of alcohol, the legal age is twenty-one (21) years of age. (See Code Section 2.015).

Louisiana: An individual may not be considered to reach an age of majority until a specific time under state law; however, a minor may engage in contracting for necessities and/or other items including employment. Once performance is made, payment shall be made either to or by the minor depending upon whether the payment or whether the benefits to the contract are received or given by the minor. A parent cannot collect a second time when payment has been made to a minor for a service such as an employment service when rendered. A minor may, however, repudiate a contract within a reasonable time after reaching majority. The legal age or age of majority in the state of Louisiana is eighteen (18) years old. (See Civil Code [CC Article 29].)

Maine: An individual may not be considered to reach an age of majority until a specific time under state law; however, a minor may engage in contracting for necessities and/or other items including employment. Once performance is made, payment shall be made either to or by the minor depending upon whether the payment or whether the benefits to the contract are received or given by the minor. A parent cannot collect a second time when payment has been made to a minor for a service such as an employment service when rendered. A minor may, however, repudiate a contract within a reasonable time after reaching majority. In the state of Maine, the legal age to contract is the age of eighteen (18). (See Section 34-A, §9004[6].) A minor in the state of Maine is anyone who has not reached the age of eighteen (18). The effective date of this enactment was January 15, 1984.

Maryland: An individual may not be considered to reach an age of majority until a specific time under state law; however, a minor may engage in contracting for necessities and/or other items including employment. Once performance is made, payment shall be made either to or by the minor depending upon whether the payment or whether the benefits to the contract are received or given by the minor. A parent cannot collect a second time when payment has been made to a minor for a service such as an employment service when rendered. A minor may, however, repudiate a contract within a reasonable time after reaching majority. The legal age for contracting in the state of Maryland is eighteen (18) years of age. (See 1, §24.) Section 3-209 prohibits employment under the age of fourteen (14), and Section 3-211 regulates employment for minors under the age of sixteen (16). The legal defense of a minority as to contracting may be asserted by a person under the age of eighteen (18). This, however, may be somewhat contrary to the general rules governing contracts and minors in Maryland. It implies that no one other than a minor may assert this defense on the minor's behalf and that a person who makes a contract while a minor may not assert the defense on his own behalf at any time after he has reached the age of majority. But then, on the other hand, the general rule in Maryland has been that if a contract made by a minor is not beneficial to him or her, the contract is void and ab initio. Also, if it is of uncertain nature, it is voidable only at the election of the minor. In regard to voidable contracts, a minor may disaffirm the contract either reaching his minority or unless ratified by him, within a reasonable time after he has obtained his majority. Voidable contracts may also be disaffirmed by the minor's privies in blood.

Massachusetts: An individual may not be considered to reach an age of majority until a specific time under state law; however, a minor may engage in contracting for necessities and/or other items including employment. Once performance is made, payment shall be made either to or by the minor depending upon whether the payment or whether the benefits to the contract are received or given by the minor. A parent cannot collect a second time when payment has been made to a minor for a service such as an employment service when rendered. A minor may, however, repudiate a contract within a reasonable time after reaching majority. In the Commonwealth of Massachusetts, the age of legal capacity is eighteen (18) years (Massachusetts Code 231:85P). Other age limitations relate to various acts including criminal acts and the treatment of individuals under eighteen (18) years of age. For information relating to such treatment, see *Lawchek Criminal Law*,

Massachusetts. There are other exceptions and features relative to minors, including business or dealing in the state of Massachusetts as minors; however, the age of legal capacity is eighteen (18) years.

Michigan: An individual may not be considered to reach an age of majority until a specific time under state law; however, a minor may engage in contracting for necessities and/or other items including employment. Once performance is made, payment shall be made either to or by the minor depending upon whether the payment or whether the benefits to the contract are received or given by the minor. A parent cannot collect a second time when payment has been made to a minor for a service such as an employment service when rendered. A minor may, however, repudiate a contract within a reasonable time after reaching majority. The legal age of majority in Michigan is eighteen (18) years. The most current Age of Majority Act was passed in 1971, and relevant code sections may be found at 722.51 et. seq. Minor is also defined in the Michigan Probate Code at Section 700.8 to be a person less than eighteen (18) years of age.

Minnesota: The legal age in the state of Minnesota is eighteen (18) years of age for both males and females. (See Sections 45.451.) However, individuals who are under the age of eighteen (18) may engage in certain contracts including real estate contracts (Section 507.02). An individual under the age of eighteen (18) is liable for all cost of necessities through any contracts made for such necessities; however, any contracts other than for necessities are voidable and subject to rescission by an individual under the age of eighteen (18). In order for an individual under the age of eighteen (18) to engage in the litigation process, such individual must be represented by a guardian ad litem if under fourteen (14), otherwise, by general guardian or relative or next of friend.

Mississippi: An individual may not be considered to reach an age of majority until a specific time under state law; however, a minor may engage in contracting for necessities and/or other items including employment. Once performance is made, payment shall be made either to or by the minor depending upon whether the payment or whether the benefits to the contract are received or given by the minor. A parent cannot collect a second time when payment has been made to a minor for a service such as an employment service when rendered. A minor may, however, repudiate a contract within a reasonable time after reaching majority. The legal age in the state of Mississippi is eighteen (18) years and older. Before one is considered competent to contract, they must be eighteen (18) years or older; however, that does not mean that people under the age of eighteen (18) years of age may not be able to contract under certain circumstances. (See Section 93-19-13.)

Missouri: An individual may not be considered to reach an age of majority until a specific time under state law; however, a minor may engage in contracting for necessities and/or other items including employment. Once performance is made, payment shall be made either to or by the minor depending upon whether the payment or whether the benefits to the contract are received or given by the minor. A parent cannot collect a second time when payment has been made to a minor for a service such as an employment service when rendered. A minor may, however, repudiate a contract within a reasonable time after reaching majority. The accepted legal age for contracting in the state of Missouri is eighteen (18) years of age. (See Code Section 431.055.) Individuals under the age of eighteen (18) may contract under certain circumstances.

Montana: An individual may not be considered to reach an age of majority until a specific time under state law; however, a minor may engage in contracting for necessities and/or other items including employment. Once performance is made, payment shall be made either to or by the minor depending upon whether the payment or whether the benefits to the contract are received or given by the minor. A parent cannot collect a second time when payment has been made to a minor for a service such as an employment service when rendered. A minor may, however, repudiate a contract within a reasonable time after reaching majority. The legal age to officially contract in the state of Montana is eighteen (18) years of age. (See Code Section 41-1-101.) Individuals under certain circumstances may contract prior to reaching the age of eighteen (18).

Nebraska: An individual may not be considered to reach an age of majority until a specific time under state law; however, a minor may engage in contracting for necessities and/or other items including employment. Once performance is made, payment shall be made either to or by the minor depending upon whether the payment or whether the benefits to the contract are received or given by the minor. A parent cannot collect a second time when payment has been made to a minor for a service such as an employment service when rendered. A minor may, however, repudiate a contract within a reasonable time after reaching majority. In Nebraska, all persons under nineteen (19) years of age are declared to be minors. In cases in which any person marries under the age of nineteen (19) years, his or her minority ends. (See Code Section 43.2101 of Nebraska laws.)

Nevada: The legal age in the state of Nevada is the age of eighteen (18). Anyone under the age of eighteen (18) is considered an infant, unless sixteen (16) years or older and emancipated by a court of law. (See Code Section 129.010.) For emancipation to occur in Nevada, a person must be at least sixteen (16) years of age and must receive an order by a District Court in the county of the minor's residence that states the sixteen (16) year old is a party who has been declared to be emancipated. Once a court provides such a declaration, the decree serves to remove all indications that the individual is a minor. Accordingly, anyone who has been emancipated who has reached the age of eighteen (18) may incur a legal indebtedness or a contractual obligation without the right of rescission. Such individual may also bring a cause of action through the legal process in their own name and may settle their own disputes. Such individuals, either those emancipated or reaching the age of eighteen (18), may acquire, encumber or convey property without the signature of a consenting adult. Emancipation, as well as reaching the age of eighteen (18), allows the individual to consent to their own medical, dental, and psychiatric care, as well as, establish their own school enrollment and residence.

In the state of Nevada, minors are prohibited from purchasing or consuming alcoholic beverages or possessing alcoholic beverages if they are under the age of twenty-one (21) years. If the individual is under the age of eighteen (18), he or she may not purchase cigarettes.

New Hampshire: The age of majority, or the legal age, in the state of New Hampshire is eighteen (18) years of age. The effective date of this legislation is June 3, 1973. For the consumption of alcohol beverages, the legal age is twenty-one (21) years of age. (See Chapter 175, Section 6.) Individuals under the age of majority or, in other words, under the age of eighteen (18), have the right to contract under certain circumstances and in certain cases may rescind the contracts. Individuals under the age of eighteen (18) may also be stockholders in corporations, as well as, in building and loan associations and/or credit unions. Parents are not responsible for the negligent acts of children unless the parents themselves are independently negligent. Under certain circumstances, however, the parents or guardians may be ordered to make restitution to victims for acts caused by minors. (See Code Chapter 169B, Section 45; see also Chapter 507, Section 8-e.) In order to bring an action in court, a minor must use a next of friend. The next of friend is generally a parent. In any settlements which exceed $10,000, the court must approve such settlements.

New Jersey: The legal age in the state of New Jersey is eighteen (18) years of age for both males and females. However, it is possible for individuals under the age of eighteen (18) to contract and if so, they may ratify their contracts once reaching majority or, in other words, the age of eighteen(18). Any ratification of contract obligation should be in writing. For real estate transactions of individuals who are under the age of eighteen (18), it would be necessary for a guardian or guardian ad litem, or a person having invested interest in the land, to join in the conveyance of anyone under the age of eighteen (18). In regard to obtaining the age of majority, see Title 9, Chapter 17B, Section 4.

New Mexico: In New Mexico, the legal age or age of majority is age eighteen (18); however, the age of twenty-one (21) is required for the purchase of alcoholic beverages. (See Section 28-6-1 of the New Mexico statute.) An individual may become an emancipated individual by virtue of marriage. It should be noted that a married minor may join with a spouse in all conveyances, mortgages, leases, etc., with the same effect as though the minor spouse had obtained majority. (See Section 40-3-15.) Individuals under the age of eighteen (18) may contract for various needs and employment; however, they have the right of ratification of those contracts when reaching the age of majority.

New York: The legal age or age of majority in New York is eighteen (18) years for both men and women. (See Domestic Relations Law, Section 2.) However, individuals under the age of twenty-one (21) may not consume or procure alcoholic beverages pursuant to Section 65, Alcohol Beverage Control Law. Individuals under the age of eighteen (18) may contract; however, those individuals may disaffirm most contracts after reaching the age of majority. There are certain loans, the acquisition of medical care, and insurance that may be contracted below the age of eighteen (18). Also, athletes and artists under the age of eighteen (18) may contract for their services. If an individual is under eighteen (18) and married, he or she may contract for the purchase of a home without the disaffirmance after reaching majority.

North Carolina: In the state of North Carolina, the legal age is eighteen (18) years of age. (See General Statutes of the state of North Carolina, Chapter 48A-1 and 48A-2.) However, for the purchase of liquor, mixed beverages and wine, the legal age is age twenty-one (21). (See General Statutes of North Carolina, Section 18B-302[b][2].)

An individual under the age of eighteen (18) may become emancipated upon marriage. A minor, age sixteen (16) years or older, may petition the court for a Decree of Emancipation. (See Chapter 7A, 717 to 726.) Minors (individuals under the age of eighteen [18] or individuals who were not emancipated) may contract and are permitted to ratify their contract by silence for a reasonable time, such as three (3) years after obtaining the age of majority. In situations involving medical care, the minor may consent to have medical treatment without first getting the approval of a parent/guardian under certain conditions.

North Dakota: The legal age in the state of North Dakota is the age of eighteen (18). However, the legal age for drinking is the age of twenty-one (21). A parent in the state of North Dakota may relinquish to a child, the right of control and may also relinquish to the child, the child's right to earnings. (See Section 14-09-17 of the North Dakota Century Code.) In North Dakota, a parent is responsible for a minor's negligent operation of a motor vehicle. (See Section 39-06-09.) However, a parent is not liable for other torts of minors and other civil liability incurred by minors. (See Section 14-10-03 of the North Dakota Century Code.) Minors under the age of eighteen (18) may contract; however, they may disaffirm those contracts either before becoming of legal age or within one (1) year after becoming legal age. (See Section 14-10-11, North Dakota Century Code.) However, a minor may not disaffirm a contract for a reasonable value of support received.

Ohio: The legal age in the state of Ohio is eighteen (18) years of age. (See Section 3109.01 of the Ohio Revised Code.) In regard to intoxicating beverages, the age of twenty-one (21) is required (Section 4301.63 and 4301.632).

There are some restrictions regarding the employment of individuals under the age of eighteen (18) years. Individuals under the age of eighteen (18) may contract relative to performance of legal duty and for the purchase of necessity; however, those contracts may be voidable at the decision of the individual who may disaffirm the contracts within a reasonable period of time after reaching the age of eighteen (18).

Oklahoma: The legal age in the state of Oklahoma is the age of eighteen (18). (See Section 15-13 Oklahoma Statutes.) For alcoholic beverages of $1^1/_2$ of 1 percent alcohol by volume, the legal age is twenty-one (21) years of age. (See Section 37-537 of the Oklahoma Statutes.) An individual under the age of eighteen (18) who is legally married may dispose of and contract relating to real estate acquired after marriage. However, an individual under the age of eighteen (18) may own real estate. (See Section 16-32 of the Oklahoma Statutes.)

An individual under the age of eighteen (18) may not disaffirm a contract for necessities or obligations entered by expressed authority or by statute. (See Sections 15-20 and 15-21 of the Oklahoma Statutes.) As to other contracts, a minor within one (1) year of reaching his age of majority or being emancipated may disaffirm any other contracts that he has formed.

Oregon: The legal age in the state of Oregon is eighteen (18) years of age. However, a person may become emancipated upon marriage. (See Section 109.510 and 109.520 of the Oregon Revised Statutes.) In Oregon, the age of majority as to gifts is the age of twenty-one (21). (See Section 126.805[1].) Also in Oregon, an individual who is under eighteen (18) years of age may be emancipated by parental act or by decree.

Individuals under the age of eighteen (18) may engage in contracts for necessities including residential dwelling units and for utility services. (See Section 109.697 of the Oregon Revised Statutes.) Individuals under the age of eighteen (18) are also obligated for educational loans pursuant to Section 348.105 of the Oregon Revised Statutes. As to other contracts in the state of Oregon, those contracts may be voided upon an individual reaching the age of eighteen (18) or being otherwise emancipated. However, if the contract was fair and the minor received benefits, then the value which was received must be returned.

Pennsylvania: In Pennsylvania, the legal age refers to any person under the age of twenty-one (21). (See Pennsylvania Consolidated Statutes 1* 1991.) In matters of probate, estates, and fiduciaries, a minor is defined to be a person who is under the age of eighteen (18) except as in regard to the Uniform Transfers to Minors Act. (See the Pennsylvania Consolidated Statute 20*102,5301.)

Generally, individuals under the age of twenty-one (21) may be able to void a contract upon reaching legal age, except for contracts of necessities. However, individuals eighteen (18) years of age or more may engage in binding and legally enforceable contracts. (See Pennsylvania Consolidated Statutes 23*5101.) Under certain circumstances, individuals who have obtained the age of eighteen (18) and have graduated from high school or who are married or have been pregnant may engage in medical contracts or contracts of necessity. Individuals seventeen (17) years of age or older may enter into contracts involving certain loans.

Rhode Island: In Rhode Island, the legal age is the age of eighteen (18) for both men and women. (See Section 15-12-1.) However, an individual must be twenty-one (21) years of age or older in order to purchase or consume alcoholic beverages. (See Section 3-8-1 through 3-8-11.4.) Additionally, an individual must be eighteen (18) years of age or older in order to purchase tobacco products. (See Section 11-9-13.) Under certain circumstances, individuals under the age of eighteen (18) may engage and be a part of a contract and may negotiate contractual rights.

South Carolina: The legal age in the state of South Carolina is the age of eighteen (18) for both males and females. However, an individual must be twenty-one (21) years or older to purchase beer, wine, or any form of alcoholic beverage. Individuals under the age of eighteen (18) may contract for necessities and may otherwise contract; however, said individual would have until age of majority to ratify the contracts that were made by them while a minor. Ratification should be in writing. (See Section 20-7-240 of the Code of Laws of South Carolina.) An exception to this regulation may relate to the borrowing of money as to expenses of attending any educational institution. The employment of minors must be with the consent of adults, except where the parent or guardian fails or refuses to furnish a home in support. (See Section 41-13-40 Code of Laws of South Carolina.)

South Dakota: In South Dakota, the legal age for individuals is the age of eighteen (18). This is true for both men and women. (See Section 26-1-1 of South Dakota Codified Laws.) The drinking age of alcoholic beverages is the age of twenty-one (21). Parents of minors may agree to an emancipation of an individual under the age of eighteen (18). (See Section 25-5-19.) Also, a minor may be emancipated if the minor enters into a valid marriage, is on active duty with the armed services, or is declared emancipated under the courts. (See Section 25-5-24 of the South Dakota Codified Laws.) Recision or avoiding of a declaration of emancipation does not alter a contractual obligation arising during the period the declaration of emancipation is in effect. (See Section 25-5-27 of the South Dakota Codified Laws.) The minor may contract and is bound to the contract under Section 26-2-1, unless the contract is disaffirmed as permitted by law. (See Section 26-2-6.)

Tennessee: The legal age in Tennessee is the age of eighteen (18) for both men and women. However, as to the purchase of alcoholic beverages, the legal age is twenty-one (21) years of age. (See Section 1-3-113 of the Tennessee Code.) In Tennessee, there is no provision for emancipation of an individual by virtue of marriage. However, a court may decree that an individual is no longer to be a minor for specific purposes. (See Section 29-31-104 of the Tennessee Code.)

An individual under the age of eighteen (18) may engage in contracts; however, such individual may disaffirm the contracts, other than a contract for necessities, within a reasonable time after reaching the age of majority. An individual may ratify contracts, especially those made as a minor, once reaching majority.

Texas: The legal age or the age of majority in Texas is eighteen (18) for both men and women. However, a minor who is at least sixteen (16) years old and who lives apart from his or her parents or guardian and who is self-supporting may petition to have the minority designation removed and become emancipated. (See Section 31.01 of the Family Code of Texas.) Individuals who are married become emancipated. (See Section 4.03 of the Family Code of Texas.)

Once an individual has reached the age of majority, he or she may confirm or disaffirm contracts into which he or she has entered while a minor. Otherwise, minors may contract in the state of Texas.

Utah: Legal age in the state of Utah is eighteen (18) years for both men and women. However, a minor may obtain his or her majority by marriage. (See Section 15-2-1 of the Utah Code.) A minor may contract and is bound for the reasonable value of necessities and bound by his other contracts, unless at legal age he disaffirms those contracts within a reasonable period of time. (See Section 15-2-2 of the Utah Code.)

Vermont: The legal age in Vermont is the age of eighteen (18) for both males and females. (See Section 1-173 of the Vermont Statues.) An individual may become emancipated by virtue of marriage. The legal drinking age in Vermont is twenty-one (21). An individual under the age of eighteen (18) may contract for virtually any purpose; however, any contract made by a person under the age of eighteen (18) is violable. If a minor receives benefits and seeks to avoid the contract, then restitution of the benefits received must be paid by the minor upon disaffirming of the contract.

Virginia: The legal age in the state of Virginia is eighteen (18) years of age. (See Section 1-13.42 of the Code of Virginia.) Alcoholic beverages may not be consumed by anyone unless he or she is twenty-one (21) years of age. Individuals under the age of eighteen (18) may engage in contracts; however, they may act to void the contract once reaching the age of majority. Under specific circumstances, individuals under the age of eighteen (18) may become depositors and hold checking accounts in banks, may insure their own lives, and may create valid liens for money borrowed providing they are not less than fifteen (15) years of age. Certain other legal rights exist for minors in the state of Virginia relating to marriage, college education, etc.

Washington: The legal age in the state of Washington is eighteen (18) years of age for both men and women. (See Section 26.28.010 of the Revised Code of Washington.) A person who is married is considered to be emancipated or of legal age. (See Section 26.28.020 of the Revised Code of Washington.) Normally, an individual must be eighteen (18) years old or older in order to enter into a contract. Minors may engage in contracts for necessities and other contracts; however, they have a reasonable period of time after reaching the age of eighteen (18) to rescind those contracts. If a contract is rescinded and the individual under the age of eighteen (18) has received benefits, then the individual receiving those benefits must pay back any money or property received by virtue of the contract. (See Section 26.28.030 of the Revised Code of Washington.)

West Virginia: The legal age in the state of West Virginia is eighteen (18) years for both men and women. (See Chapter 2, Article 3, Section 1 of the West Virginia Code.) Individuals under the age of twenty-one (21) may not consume alcoholic beverages. If an individual under the age of eighteen (18) and over the age of sixteen (16) can establish that he or she is capable of his or her own support, he or she may petition to the court for their own emancipation. Once emancipated, an individual has all of the rights and privileges of an individual of full age. Individuals under the age of eighteen (18) may contract; however, ratification of the contracts is required and must be in writing. (See Chapter 55, Article 1, Section 1 of the West Virginia Code.)

Wisconsin: The legal age in the state of Wisconsin is the age of eighteen (18) for both men and women. (See Section 990.01[3] of the Wisconsin Statutes.) In Wisconsin, an individual may contract under the age of eighteen (18); however, he is not responsible or liable for the contracts made while a minor except for necessity. However, a minor may reaffirm and ratify contracts that were made under the legal age once the individual reaches the age of majority or passes the age of eighteen (18). If an individual marries in the state of Wisconsin under the age of eighteen (18), that individual becomes emancipated and has recognition as an adult. (See Section 880.04[1] of the Wisconsin Statutes.)

Wyoming: The legal age in the state of Wyoming is eighteen (18) years for both men and women. (See Section 14-1-101 of the Wyoming Statutes.) Individuals may become emancipated once they become married or become a member of the military service or if they have received a decree of emancipation from the courts pursuant to Section 14-1-201 and 14-1-203. Individuals under the age of eighteen (18) may contract; however, they have until they have reached the age of majority to ratify or rescind the contract. When legally married, a minor may consent to health-care treatment to the same extent as if they are an adult. A minor may also consent to health-care treatment if in inactive military service or when the parents or guardian of the child cannot be reached with due diligence.

What is the commercial code?

The Uniform Commercial Code was developed to allow each state to adopt a uniform system of regulating various items that were often the subject of contracts throughout the United States. The intent of the draft was to provide a uniform system of contracting and, in the process, most Uniform Commercial Codes of various states include specific statements and rules relative to sales; leases; negotiable instruments; bank deposits; collections; funds transfers; letters of credit; warehouse receipts; bills of lading; documents of title; investment securities; and secured transactions, including sales of account, contract rights, and chattel paper. The Uniform Commercial Code has evolved over the years, and each state has its own specific breakdown and particular emphasis on portions of the Uniform Commercial Code that relate to contracting in that particular state.

Alabama: In Alabama, the Uniform Commercial Code is found under Title 7 and is titled Commercial Code. It became effective in present form in 1992 and is broken down into twelve articles: Article 1—General Provisions; Article 2—Sales; Article 2A—Leases; Article 3—Commercial Paper; Article 4—Bank Deposits and Collections; Article 4A—Funds Transfers; Article 5—Letters of Credit; Article 6—Bulk Transfers; Article 7—Warehouse Receipts, Bills of Lading and Other Documents of Title; Article 8—Investment Securities; Article 9—Secured Transactions, Sales of Accounts and Chattel Paper; Article 10—Effective Date and Repealer; and Article 11—Effective Date and Transition.

Alaska: Title 45 of Trade and Commerce under the Alaska Code is known as the Uniform Commercial Code. Its date of enactment or its effective date was January 1, 1994. Title 45 is divided into various chapters, including the following: Chapter 1—General Provisions; Chapter 2—Sales; Chapter 3—Negotiable Instruments; Chapter 4—Bank Deposits and Collections; Chapter 5—Letters of Credit; Chapter 7—Warehouse Receipts, Bills of Lading, and Other Documents of Title; Chapter 8—Investment Securities; Chapter 9—Secured Transactions, Sales of Accounts, Contract Rights, and Chattel Paper; Chapter 10—Alaska Retail Installment Sales Act; Chapter 12—Leases;

Chapter 14—Funds Transfers; Chapter 20—Purchase of Ore; Chapter 30—Sales of Mobile Homes; Chapter 45—Trade Practices; Chapter 50—Competitive Practices and Regulation of Competition; Chapter 55—Alaska Securities Act of 1959; Chapter 57—Takeover Bid Disclosure Act; Chapter 63—Telephone Solicitations; Chapter 65—Handicrafts and Works of Art; Chapter 68—Charitable Solicitations; Chapter 70—Sureties; Chapter 75—Weights and Measures Act; Chapter 77—Foreign Trade Zones; Chapter 88—Alternative Energy Revolving Loan Fund; Chapter 89—Residential Energy Conservation Fund; Chapter 90—Tourism Revolving Fund; Chapter 92—Fishery Product Revolving Loan Guarantee Fund; Chapter 94—Forest Products Business Loan Guarantee Program; Chapter 95—Small Business Loans; and Chapter 98—Historical District Loan Act.

Arizona: The Uniform Commercial Code was a uniform law drafted by the National Conference of Commissions on Uniform State Laws and American Law Institute Governing Commercial Transaction. The Uniform Commercial Code was adopted in Arizona on February 20, 1967. The effective date for the Uniform Commercial Code in Arizona was January 1, 1968. It was principally designed to regulate sales and the leasing of goods, along with the transfer of funds, commercial paper, and bank deposits and collections. Additionally, its design includes the regulation of letters of credit, warehouse receipts, bills of lading, investment securities, and secured transactions.

Arkansas: The Uniform Commercial Code in the state of Arkansas is covered under Chapters 27 through 97 in Volume 22B and is titled Business and Commercial Law. Subtitle One is Uniform Commercial Code and is broken down into the following chapters: Chapter 1—General Provisions; Chapter 2—Sales; Chapter 3—Negotiable Instruments; Chapter 4—Bank Deposits and Collections; Chapter 4A—Funds/Transfers; Chapter 5—Letters of Credit; Chapter 6—Bulk Transfers; Chapter 7—Warehouse Receipts, Bills of Lading and Other Documents of Title; Chapter 8—Investment Securities; Chapter 9—Secured Transactions, Sales of Accounts, Contract Rights, and Chattel Paper; and Chapter 10—Effective Date and Repealer.

California: The Uniform Commercial Code of the state of California is broken down into twelve chapters. Chapter 1 relates to title, construction, location, and subject matter. Chapter 1 also relates to general definitions and principals of interpretation, and its initial Section is 1201. Chapter 2 deals in sales with its initial section as 2101 with the title General Construction Subject Matter; Form, Formation, and Readjustment commences at Section 2201; General Obligation and Construction of Contract commences at Section 2301; Title Creditors and Good Faith Purchasers commences at Section 2401; Performance commences at Section 2501; Breach, Repudiation and Excuse commences at Section 2601; and Remedies commences at Section 2701. Chapter 3, dealing with commercial paper, commences at Section 3101 and is broken down with the following: Short Title, Form, and Interpretation, commencing at 3101; Transfer and Negotiation, commencing at 3201; Rights of a Holder, commencing at Section 3301; Liability of Parties, commencing at Section 3401; Presentation, Notice of Dishonor and Protest, commencing at Section 3501; Discharge, commencing at Section 3601; Advice of International Sight Draft, commencing at Section 3701; and Miscellaneous, commencing at Section 3801. Chapter 4, dealing with bank deposits and collections, begins at Section 4101 and is broken down as follows: General Provisions and Definitions, commencing at Section 4101; Collection of Items Including Depository and Collecting Banks, commencing at Section 4201; Collection of Items Including Payor Banks, commencing at Section 4301; Relationship between Payor Bank and Its Customers, commencing at Section 4401; and Collection of Documentary Drafts, commencing at Section 4501. Chapter 5 deals with letters of credit and commences at Section 5101. Bulk Transfer is found in Chapter 6 and commences at Section 6101. Chapter 7 deals with warehouse receipts, bills of lading, and other documents of title and commences at Section 7101. The bulk transfer portion no longer applies. Chapter 8 deals with investment securities and commences at Section 8101. Secured Transactions including Sales of Accounts, Contract Rights and Chattel Paper commences at Section 9101. The Effective Date and Repealer is found in Chapter 10. The Effective Date and Transition Provision are found in Chapters 11 and 12.

Colorado: The Uniform Commercial Code in the state of Colorado is found under Title 4. For the various code sections, see 4-1-101 et. seq. The Uniform Commercial Code was adopted in 1987 in the state of Colorado. The Uniform Commercial Code in Colorado is broken down into twelve articles. Those articles include the following: Article 1—General Provisions; Article 2—Sales; Article 3—Commercial Paper; Article 4—Bank Deposits and Collections; Article 5—Letters of Credit; Article 6—Bulk Transfers; Article 7—Warehouse Receipts, Bills of Lading, and Other Documents; Article 8—Investment Securities; Article 9—Secured Transactions; Article 9.5—Central Filing of Effective Financial Statements; Article 10—Effective Date; and Article 11—Fees.

Connecticut: The Uniform Commercial Code in the state of Connecticut is found under Title 42a. It became effective in 1959. Article 1 of Title 42 deals with general provisions. Article 2 deals with sales, and Sales is divided into various subparts. Those subparts are addressed at this juncture in relationship to contracts. Part 1 deals with the short title and general construction and subject matter and is titled Uniform Commercial Code—Sales and is found under Section 42a-2-101. The General Obligation and Construction of a contract may be found under Part 3 commencing at 42a-2-301. Matters dealing with title, creditors, and good faith purchases are under Part 4 and Part 5, while Part 5 deals with performance. Part 6 deals with breach, repudiation and excuse, and Part 7 deals with remedies. For the remaining portions of the Uniform Commercial Code in the state of Connecticut, see Title 42a.

Delaware: The Uniform Commercial Code is one of the uniform laws drafted by the National Conference of Commissioners on Uniform State Laws and the American Law Institute Governing Commercial Transactions. Its intent is to govern sales, leasing of goods, transfer of funds, commercial paper, bank deposits and collections, letters of credit, warehouse receipts, bills of lading, investment securities, and secured transactions.

Florida: The Uniform Commercial Code in the state of Florida may be found under Chapters 670 et. seq. Chapter 670 is the Uniform Commercial Code relative to Article 4A—Funds Transfers; Chapter 671—Uniform Commercial Code, Article 1, deals with general provisions; Chapter 672—Uniform Commercial Code, Article 2, deals with sales. Each of the foregoing chapters is found in Volume 1. In Volume 1a, the contents of the Uniform Commercial Code may be found: Chapter 673—Uniform Commercial Code (Article 3—Negotiable Instruments); Chapter 674—Uniform Commercial Code (Article 4—Bank Deposits and Collections); Chapter 675—Uniform Commercial Code (Article 5—Letters of Credit); Chapter 677—Uniform Commercial Code (Article 7—Warehouse Receipts, Bills of Lading, and Other Documents of Title); Chapter 678—Uniform Commercial Code (Article 8—Investment Securities). In Volume 2, the following portions of the Uniform Commercial Code may be found: Chapter 679—Uniform Commercial Code (Article 9—Secured Transactions, Sales of Accounts, and Chattel Paper); and Chapter 680—Uniform Commercial Code (Article 2A—Leases).

Georgia: The Uniform Commercial Code in the state of Georgia is found as Title 109A. The Uniform Commercial Code is divided into eleven articles, and the code was adopted in 1962. The effective date of the act was postponed until April 1, 1963. In 1963, the act was amended and was further postponed until the effective date of January 1, 1964. The Uniform Commercial Code in Georgia includes the following: Article 1—General Provisions; Article 2—Sales; Article 3—Commercial Paper; Article 4—Bank Deposits and Collections; Article 5—Letters of Credit; Article 6—Bulk Transfers; Article 7—Warehouse Receipts, Bills of Lading, and Other Documents of Title; Article 8—Investment Securities; Article 9—Secured Transactions, Sales of Account, and Chattel Paper; Article 10—Effective Date of Repealer; and Article 11—Effective Date and Transition Provisions. Article 11 also includes revised Article 9—Conforming Amendments to Other Articles.

Hawaii: The Uniform Commercial Code in Hawaii is regulated pursuant to Title 27, Chapter 490. (See Sections 490:1-101 to 490:11-108 in particular.) The following articles should be noted: Article 1—General Provisions; Article 2—Sales; Article 2A—Leases; Article 3—Negotiable Instruments; Article 4—Bank Deposits and Collections; Article 4A—Funds Transfers; Article 5—Letters of Credit; Article 6—Bulk Sales; Article 7—Warehouse Receipts, Bills of Lading, and Other Documents of Title; Article 8—Investment Securities; Article 9—Secured Transactions, Sales of Accounts, Contract Rights, and Chattel Paper; and Article 10—the Effective Date and Repealer.

Idaho: The Uniform Commercial Code in Idaho is governed pursuant to Title 28. The code is divided into ten sections, including the following: Chapter 1—General Provisions; Chapter 2—Sales; Chapter 3—Commercial Paper; Chapter 4—Bank Deposits and Collections; Chapter 5—Letters of Credit; Chapter 6—Bulk Transfers; Chapter 7—Warehouse Receipts, Bills of Lading, and Other Documents of Title; Chapter 8—Investment Securities; Chapter 9—Secured Transactions and Other Sales of Accounts, Contract Rights, and Chattel Paper; and Chapter 10—Effective Date and Repealer.

Illinois: In Illinois, the Uniform Commercial Code is found under Chapter 810. The Illinois Commercial Code is divided into the following articles: Article 1—General Provisions; Article 2—Sales; Article 2A—Leases; Article 3—Negotiable Instruments; Article 4—Bank Deposits and Collections; Article 4A—Funds Transfers; Article 5—Letters of Credit; Article 6—Bulk Transfers (which has been repealed); Article 7—Warehouse Receipts, Bills of Lading, and Other Documents of Title; Article 8—Investment Securities; Article 9—Secured Transactions: Sales of Account, Contract Rights, and Chattel Paper; Article 10—Effective Date and Repealer; Article 11—Effective Date and Transition Amendatory Act of 1972; and Article 12—Effective Date and Transition Amendatory Act of 1987. Article 1 under General Provisions provides for general definitions and principals of interpretation. Particular attention is drawn to Section 5/1-202, which provides general definitions. Article 2 is devoted to sales and is broken down into seven subparts, which include Part 1—General Construction and Subject Matter; Part 2—Form, Formation, and Readjustment of Contract; Part 3—General Obligation and Construction of Contract; Part 4—Title Creditors and Good Faith Purchasers; Part 5—Performance; Part 6—Breach, Repudiation, and Excuse; and Part 7—Remedies. Article 3 relates to negotiable instruments and includes eight parts, including Part 1—General Definitions; Part 2—Negotiation and Endorsement; Part 3—Enforcement of Instruments; Part 4—Liability of Parties; Part 5—Dishonor; Part 6—Discharge and Payment; Part 7—Advice of International Sight Draft; and Part 8—Miscellaneous. Article 4 relates to bank deposits and collections. Article 4 also includes five subparts. The five subparts are broken down into Part 1—General Provisions and Definitions; Part 2—Collection of Items: Depository and Collecting Banks; Part 3—Collection of Items; Payor Banks; Part 4—Relationship Between Payor Banks and Customers; and Part 5—Collection of Documentary Drafts. Article 5 deals with letters of credit, and Article 6, which dealt with bulk transfers, was repealed on January 1, 1992. Bulk Sales Transfers was brought into existence due to potential fraud that may have occurred when a merchant would sell inventory and abscond with the proceeds leaving certain creditors unpaid. To some limited extent, the law of fraudulent conveyances ameliorated the creditor's plight. Other legislation is also used to rectify such problems; therefore, bulk transfer regulations were no longer necessary. Thus, the law was repealed. Article 7 deals with warehouse receipts, bills of lading, and other documents of title. Article 8 deals with investment securities. Secured transactions are governed under Article 9, and such transactions include sales of accounts, contract rights, and chattel paper.

Indiana: The Uniform Commercial Code or the Commercial Law in Indiana is found in Title 26. In Title 26, the Uniform Commercial Code is known as Article 1. It deals with all commercial transactions and is broken down into the following nine chapters: Chapter 1 of the Uniform Commercial Code of Indiana relates to general provisions; Chapter 2 of the Uniform Commercial Code relates to sales; Chapter 3 relates to commercial paper; Chapter 4 relates to bank deposits and collections; Chapter 5 relates to letters of credit; Chapter 6 was written for bulk transfers; Chapter 7 is written relative to warehouse receipts, bills of lading, and other documents of title; Chapter 8 is written for investment securities; and Chapter 9 is written for secured transactions. Each of these chapters is then broken down into various sections that govern commercial transactions in the state of Indiana.

Iowa: The Uniform Commercial Code in the state of Iowa is found under Chapter 554 of the Code of Iowa. The major sections of the Uniform Commercial Code, which are designed for convenience, consistency, and fairness, include Article I—Article; Article II—Sales (this section is subdivided into Open Price Term, Risk of Loss, Modification of a Contract, and Specific Performance); Article III—Commercial Paper (divided into Deposit Endorsements, Restrictive Endorsements and Bank Collections, Effect of Unauthorized Signature, Liability of Accommodation Party, and Time for Presentment); Article IV—Bank Deposits and Collections; Article V—Letters of Credit; Article VII—Documents of Title—Destination Bills; Article VIII—Investment Securities (including General Terminology, Registered Instruments as Negotiable and Investment Securities); Article IX—Secured Transactions (in general, use of inventory as collateral, secured line of credit, proceeds, fixtures, modification of contract, formalities of financing statement, default provisions, and forfeitures.)

Kansas: Under the Kansas statutes, the Uniform Commercial Code is found under Chapter 18. Chapter 18 is divided into the following sections: the General Provisions begin at Article 18-4, Sales at 84-2 et seq., Commercial Paper at 84-3 et seq., Bank Deposits and Collections at 84-4 et seq., Letters of Credit at 84.5 se seq., Bulk Transfers at 84.6 et seq., Warehouse Receipts at 84-7 et seq., Investment Securities at 84-8 et seq., and Secured Transactions are found at 84-9 et seq. The effective date and repealer are found at Section 84-10-101.

Kentucky: The Uniform Commercial Code in the state of Kentucky is found under Chapter 355. The Commercial Code in Kentucky is broken down into the following: Article 1—General Provisions, broken down into two parts (Part 1—Instruction Application and Subject Matter of the

Chapter and Part 2—General Definitions and Principals of Interpretation); Article 2—Sales, broken down into seven subparts (Part 1—General Construction Subject Matter; Part 2—Form, Formation and Readjustment of Contract; Part 3—General Obligations and Construction of Contract; Part 4—Title Creditors and Good Faith Purchasers; Part 5—Performance; Part 6—Breach, Repudiation, and Excuse; and Part 7—Remedies); Article 3—Commercial Paper, broken down into eight sections (Part 1—Form and Interpretation; Part 2—Transfer and Negotiation; Part 3—Rights of Holders; Part 4—Liability of Parties; Part 5—Presentment, Notice of Dishonor and Protest; Part 6—Discharge; Part 7—Advise of International Sight Draft; and Part 8—Miscellaneous); Article 4—Bank Deposits and Collections, broken down into five parts (Part 1—General Provisions and Definitions; Part 2—Collection of Items: Depository and Collecting Banks; Part 3—Collection of Items: Payor Banks; Part 4—Relationship between Payor Bank and its Customer; and Part 5—Collection of Documentary Drafts); Article 5—Letters of Credit; Article 6—Bulk Transfers; Article 7—Warehouse Receipts, Bills of Lading and Other Documents of Title, broken down into six parts (Part 1—General; Part 2—Warehouse Receipts: Special Provisions; Part 3—Bills of Lading: Special Provisions; Part 4—Warehouse Receipts and Bills of Lading: General Obligations; Part 5—Warehouse Receipts and Bills of Lading: Negotiation and Transfer; Part 6—Warehouse Receipts and Bills of Lading: Miscellaneous Provisions; Article 8—Investment Securities, broken down into four parts (Part 1—Short Title and General Matters; Part 2—Issue-Issuer; Part 3—Purchase; and Part 4—Registration); Article 9—Secured Transactions: Sales of Accounts, Contract Rights and Chattel Paper, broken down into five parts (Part 1—Short Title, Applicability, and Definitions; Part 2—Validity of Security Agreements and Rights of Parties thereto; Part 3—Rights of Third Parties, Perfected and Unperfected Security Interest, Rules of Priority; Part 4—Filing; and Part 5—Default); Article 10—other provisions; and Article 11—Transition.

Louisiana: The Commercial Code was designed for all commercial transactions in the state of Louisiana. The Uniform Commercial Code in Louisiana is divided into the following sections: Chapter 1—General Provision; Chapter 2—Sales; Chapter 3—Negotiable Instruments; Chapter 4—Bank Deposits and Collections; Chapter 4A—Funds Transfers; Chapter 5—Letters of Credit; Chapter 7—Warehouse Receipts, Bills of Lading, and Other Documents of Title; Chapter 8—Investment Securities; and Chapter 9—Secured Transactions: Sales of Accounts, and Chattel Paper.

Maine: The Uniform Commercial Code in the state of Maine is found in Title 11. It is broken down into the following Articles: Article 1—General Provisions; Article 2—Sales; Article 3—Negotiable Instruments; Article 4—Bank Deposits and Collections; Article 5—Letters of Credit; Article 6—Relating to Bulk Transfers, has been repealed; Article 7—Warehouse Receipts, Bills of Lading, and Other Documents of Title; Article 8—Investment Securities; and Article 9—Secured Transactions, Sales of Accounts, Contract Rights, and Chattel Paper. The Uniform Commercial Code is designed to regulate various contracts and the formation of contracts in the state of Maine.

Maryland: The Commercial Law in the state of Maryland involves changes which have occurred in 1972, 1981, 1989, 1990, and 1991. What formerly were various "Articles" of the Uniform Commercial Code are now called "Titles." Titles 1 through 10 of the article, which relate to Commercial Law in Maryland, were derived from the original Uniform Commercial Code. The Commercial Law of the Annotated Code of Maryland is divided into the following titles: Title 1—General Provisions; Title 2—Sales; Title 3—Commercial Paper; Title 4—Bank Deposits and Collections; Title 4A—Funds Transfers; Title 5—Letters of Credit; Title 6—Bulk Transfers; Title 7—

Warehouse Receipts, Bills of Lading, and Other Documents of Title; Title 8—Investment Securities; Title 9—Secured Transactions, Sales of Accounts, Contract Rights, and Chattel Paper; Title 10—Effective Date and Repealer; and Title 11—Trade Regulation. The Commercial Law of Maryland also includes what formerly were credit regulations and those various titles include Title 12—Credit Regulations; Title 13—Consumer Protection Act; Title 14—Miscellaneous Consumer Protection Provisions; Title 15—Debt Collection: Special Provisions; Title 16—Statutory Liens on Personal Property; Title 17—Disposition of Abandoned Property; Title 18—Bills of Lading and Warehouse Receipts: Criminal Provisions; and Title 19—Equipment Dealer Contract Act.

Massachusetts: The Uniform Commercial Code in Massachusetts is found under Chapter 106. The Massachusetts Uniform Commercial Code is divided into several subsections including the following: Article 1—General Provisions; Article 2—Sales; Article 3—Commercial Paper; Article 4—Bank Deposits and Collections; Article 5—Letters of Credit; Article 6—Bulk Transfers; Article 7—Warehouse Receipts, Bills of Lading, and Other Documents of Title; Article 8—Investment Securities; and Article 9—Secured Transactions: Sales of Accounts, and Chattel Paper. The Massachusetts Uniform Commercial Code is modeled after the standard Uniform Commercial Code with some state modifications that are particular to the Commonwealth of Massachusetts.

Michigan: The Michigan Uniform Commercial Code may be found at Section 440.1101 et. seq. of the Michigan Code. The Uniform Commercial Code is divided into several Articles including the following: Article 1—General Provisions; Article 2—Sales; Article 2A—Leases; Article 3—Negotiable Instruments; Article 4—Bank Deposits and Collections; Article 4A—Funds Transfers; Article 5—Letters of Credit; Article 6—Bulk Transfers; Article 7—Warehouse Receipts, Bills of Lading, and Other Documents of Title; Article 8—Investment Securities; and Article 9—Secured Transactions, Sales of Accounts, and Chattel Paper. The Uniform Commercial Code was one of the Uniform laws adopted by the National Conference of Commissioners on Uniform State laws and American Law Institute Governing Commercial Transactions.

Minnesota: The Uniform Commercial Code was adopted as the Uniform Law as originally drafted by the National Conference of Commissioners on Uniform State Laws and the American Law Institute regarding commercial transactions. The laws were initially drafted to include sales and leasing of goods, the transfer of funds, commercial paper, bank deposits and collections, letters of credit, bulk sales (now repealed in most states), warehouse receipts, bills of lading, investment securities, and secured transactions. The principal chapter in Minnesota is Chapter 336. The Uniform Commercial Code may be found at 336.1-101 et. seq.

Mississippi: In Mississippi, Title 75 relates to the regulation of trade, commerce, and investments. Chapters 1 through 10 of Title 75 are known as the Uniform Commercial Code and cover the following areas: Chapter 1—General Provisions; Chapter 2—Sales; Chapter 3—Commercial Property; Chapter 4—Bank Deposits and Collections; Chapter 5—Letters of Credit; Chapter 6—previously related to Bulk Transfers; Chapter 7—Documents of Title; Chapter 8—Investment Securities; Chapter 9—defines the parameters for Secured Transactions, Sales of Accounts, Contract Rights, and Chattel Paper; and Chapter 10—the Effective Date and Repealer. The Mississippi regulation of Trade and Commerce and Investments under Title 75 also involves other transactional occurrences that pertain to the Uniform Commercial Code, and those chapters include the following: Chapter 11—Effective Date and Transition Provisions; Chapter 13—Bills, Notes, and other writings; Chapter 15—Sale of Checks; Chapter 17—Interest; Chapter 19—Seals; Chapter 21—

Trusts and Combines in Restraint or Hindrance of Trade; Chapter 23—Fair Trade Laws; Chapter 25—Registration of Trademarks and Labels; Chapter 27—Weights and Measures; Chapter 29—Sale and Inspection of Food and Drugs; Chapter 31—Milk and Milk Products; Chapter 33—Meat, Food, and Poultry Regulation and Inspection; Chapter 35—Meat Inspection; Chapter 37—Operation of Frozen Food Locker Plants; Chapter 39—Sale of Baby Chicks; Chapter 40—Importation and Sale of Wild Animals; Chapter 41—Gins; Chapter 43—Farm Warehouses; Chapter 44—Grain Warehouses; Chapter 45—Commercial Feeds and Grains; Chapter 47—Commercial Fertilizers; Chapter 49—Movable Homes; Chapter 51—Water Heaters; Chapter 53—Paints, Varnishes, and Similar Materials; Chapter 55—Gasoline and Petroleum Products; Chapter 56—Antifreeze and Summer Coolants; Chapter 57—Liquefied Petroleum Gases; Chapter 59—Correspondence Courses; Chapter 61—Manufacture and Sale of Jewelry and Optical Equipment; Chapter 63—Sale of Cemetery Merchandise (and funeral services); Chapter 65—Going Out of Business Sales and Unsolicited Goods; Chapter 66—Home Solicitation Sales; Chapter 67—Loans; Chapter 69—Farm Loan Bonds; Chapter 71—Uniform Securities Law; Chapter 72—Business Takeovers; Chapter 73—Hotels and Innkeepers; Chapter 74—Youth Camps; Chapter 75—Amusements, Exhibitions, and Athletic Events; and Chapter 77—Repurchase of Inventories for Retailers Upon Termination of Contract. The foregoing list some of the more commonly used chapters of Title 75 in Mississippi.

Missouri: In Missouri, a Uniform Commercial Code is found under Title XXVI, titled Trade and Commerce. This Commercial Code is identified as Chapter 400 of Title XXVI.

Montana: The Uniform Commercial Code in the state of Montana is found under Title 30. Title 30 is divided into chapters devoted to specific topics, including the following: Chapter 1—General Provisions; Chapter 2—Sales; Chapter 2A—Leases: Chapter 3—Negotiable Instruments; Chapter 4—Bank Deposits and Collections; Chapter 4A—Funds Transfers; Chapter 5—Letters of Credit; Chapter 6—Bulk Sale Transfers (however, this item has been repealed); Chapter 7—Warehouse Receipts, Bills of Lading, and Other Documents of Title; Chapter 8—Investment Securities; Chapter 9—Secured Transactions; Chapter 10—Securities Regulations; Chapter 11—Sales; Chapter 12—Weights, Measures, Standards, and Labeling; Chapter 13—Assumed Business Names, Trademarks, and Related Rights; Chapter 14—Unfair Trade Practices and Consumer Protection; Chapter 15—Foreign-Trade Zones; and Chapter 16—Small Business Licensing Coordination.

Nebraska: The Uniform Commercial Code in Nebraska is broken down into twelve articles, which include the following: Article 1—General Provisions; Article 2—Sales; Article 2A—Leases; Article 3—Negotiable Instruments; Article 4—Bank Deposits and Collections; Article 4A—Funds Transfers; Article 5—Letters of Credit; Article 6—Bulk Transfers (repealed); Article 7—Warehouse Receipts, Bills of Lading, and Other Documents of Title; Article 8—Investment Securities; Article 9—Secured Transactions, Sales of Accounts and Chattel Paper; and Article 10—Effective Date and Repealer.

Nevada: The Uniform Commercial Code adopted by Nevada is similar to the Uniform Commercial Code drafted by the National Conference of Commissioners on Uniform State Laws and the American Law Institute of Governing Commercial Transactions. The Uniform Commercial Code as contained in Nevada is a revised statute, Sections 104.1101 through 104.9507.

New Hampshire: In New Hampshire, the Uniform Commercial Code, also known as the UCC, is one of the uniform laws that was drafted by the National Conference on Commissioners for Uniform State Laws and was adopted by New Hampshire. It may be found under Chapter 382A and became effective July 1, 1961. Its principal sections include topics involving bills and notes, sales, secured transactions, leases, liens, and other commercial transactions.

New Jersey: The Uniform Commercial Code was a uniform law drafted by the National Conference on Commissioners on Uniform State Laws and the American Law Institute Governing Commercial Transactions. It was designed to protect individuals relative to sales, leasing of goods, the transfer of funds, commercial paper, bank deposits, collections, letters of credit, warehouse receipts, bills of lading, investment securities, and secured transactions. The New Jersey Uniform Commercial Code became effective on January 1, 1963. It is found at Title 12A.

New Mexico: The Uniform Commercial Code is a body of uniform laws which was drafted by the National Conference on Commissioners on Uniform State Laws and the American Law Institute. The purpose was to govern commercial transactions including sales, leasing of goods, transfer of funds, commercial paper, bank deposits, collections, letters of credit, warehouse receipts, bills of lading, investment securities, and secured transactions. The Uniform Commercial Code was adopted by New Mexico and is found under Section 55-1-101 et. seq.

New York: The Uniform Commercial Code is one of the systems of laws that is drafted by the National Conference of Commissioners on the Uniform State Laws and the American Law Institute Governing Commercial Transactions. The purpose of a Uniform Commercial Code is to govern commercial transactions such as sales, leasing of goods, transfer of funds, commercial paper, bank deposits, collections, letters of credit, bulk transfers, warehouse receipts, bills of lading, investment securities, and secured transactions. The Uniform Commercial Code in New York was adopted April 18, 1962, and became effective September 27, 1964. The Uniform Commercial Code is abbreviated U.C.C.

North Carolina: The Uniform Commercial Code is one of the uniform laws that is drafted by the National Conference of Commissioners on the Uniform State Laws and the American Law Institute Governing Commercial Transactions. The purpose of the uniform laws, in particular the Uniform Commercial Code, was to regulate sales, the leasing of goods, transfer of funds, commercial paper, bank deposits, collections, letters of credit, warehouse receipts, bills of lading, investment securities, and secured transactions. The Uniform Commercial Code in North Carolina is found in Chapter 25 and became effective July 1, 1967.

North Dakota: The Uniform Commercial Code was a uniform law drafted by the National Conference of Commissioners on Uniform State Laws and the American Law Institute Governing Commercial Transactions. The principal purpose of the Uniform Law was to establish laws that were common regarding sales and leasing of goods, transfer of funds, commercial paper, bank deposits, collections, letters of credit, warehouse receipts, bills of lading, investment securities, and secured transactions. The Uniform Commercial Code, as adopted in North Dakota, is found under Title 14 of the North Dakota Century Code.

Ohio: The Uniform Commercial Code is a series of laws that are a part of the Uniform Laws drafted by the National Conference of Commissioners on the Uniform State Laws and the American Law Institute Governing Commercial Transactions. The purpose for the Uniform Commercial Code was to standardize and simplify transactions relating to sales, leasing of goods, transfer of funds, commercial paper, bank deposits, collections, letters of credit, warehouse receipts, bills of lading, investment securities, and investment transactions. The Uniform Commercial Code is found at Chapter 1301 through 1309 of the Ohio Revised Code. It should be noted that there is significance between the numbers of individual sections of the UCC and the sections of the Ohio Revised Code.

Oklahoma: The Uniform Commercial Code is a series of laws drafted and proposed by the National Conference of Commissioners on Uniform State Laws and the American Law Institute Governing Commercial Transactions. The purpose of the Uniform Enactment was to regulate sales, leasing of goods, transfer of funds, commercial paper, bank deposits, collections, letters of credit, warehouse receipts, bills of lading, investment securities, and secured transactions, to name a few. The Uniform Commercial Code in Oklahoma is found under Title 12A of the Oklahoma Statutes and became effective on January 1, 1963.

Oregon: The Uniform Commercial Code is a series of laws drafted by the National Conference of Commissioners on the Uniform State Laws and the American Law Institute Governing Commercial Transactions. The purpose of the common draft includes regulations regarding sales, leasing of goods, transfer of funds, commercial paper, bank deposits, collections, letters of credit, warehouse receipts, bills of lading, investment securities, and secured transactions. In Oregon, the Commercial Code was adopted on September 1, 1963.

Pennsylvania: The Uniform Commercial Code is one of the laws which was drafted by the National Conference of Commissioners on Uniform State Laws and the American Law Institute Governing Commercial Transactions. The purpose was to draft a common system of laws that principally governed sales, leasing of goods, transfer of funds, commercial paper, bank deposits, collections, letters of credit, warehouse receipts, bills of lading, investment securities, and secured transactions. The Uniform Commercial Code in Pennsylvania became effective July 1, 1954. It is a part of the Pennsylvania Consolidated Statutes and is found in Title 13.

Rhode Island: The Uniform Commercial Code is one of the uniform laws drafted by the National Conference of Commissioners on the Uniform State Laws and the American Law Institute Governing Commercial Transactions. The underlying purpose of the uniform law was to assure that all states followed certain practices relating to sales, leasing of goods, transfer of funds, commercial paper, bank deposits, collections, letters of credit, warehouse receipts, bills of lading, investment security, secured transactions, etc. The Uniform Commercial Code in Rhode Island is under Title 6A of the General Laws of Rhode Island.

South Carolina: The Uniform Commercial Code is one of the uniform laws that was drafted by the National Conference of Commissioners on Uniform State Laws and the American Law Institute Governing Commercial Transactions. The purpose of the Uniform Commercial Code was to regulate sales and leasing of goods, the transfer of funds, commercial paper, bank deposits, collections, letters of credit, warehouse receipts, bills of lading, investments securities, secured transactions, etc. In South Carolina, the Uniform Commercial Code became effective as adopted on January 1, 1968. The Uniform Commercial Code in South Carolina is found under the General Statues of South Carolina, Title 36, and may be found at 36-1-101 et. seq. of the Code of Laws of South Carolina.

South Dakota: The Uniform Commercial Code is one of the uniform laws which was drafted by the National Conference of Commissioners on the Uniform State Laws and the American Law Institute Governing Commercial Transactions. The purpose of these uniform laws is to make uniform various aspects of law including sales and leasing of goods, transfer of funds, commercial paper, bank deposits, collections, letters of credit, warehouse receipts, bills of lading, investment securities, secured transactions, etc. In South Dakota, the Uniform Commercial Code generally became effective July 1, 1967; however, some provisions had become effective July 1, 1966. In South Dakota, the Uniform Commercial Code is found under Title 57A.

Tennessee: The Uniform Commercial Code of Tennessee is one of the uniform laws drafted by the National Conference of Commissioners on Uniform State Laws and the American Law Institute Governing Commercial Transactions. The purpose of the uniform draft was to include consistency relative to sales, leasing of goods, transfer of funds, commercial paper, bank deposits, collection, letters of credit, warehouse receipts, bills of lading, investment securities, secured transactions, etc. In Tennessee, the Uniform Commercial Code may be found under Section 47-1-101 et. seq. of the Tennessee Code.

Texas: The Uniform Commercial Code is one of the uniform laws drafted by the National Conference of Commissions on Uniform State Laws and the American Law Institute Governing Commercial Transactions. It is designed to set forth common legal principles relative to sales, leasing of goods, transfer of funds, commercial paper, bank deposits, collections, letters of credit, warehouse receipts, bills of lading, investment securities, and secured transactions. (See *Black's Law Dictionary,* 1990 edition.)

In Texas, the Uniform Commercial Code is found under the Business and Commerce Code, Title 1. It was originally enacted in 1962 and amended in 1972, 1977, 1987, 1988, and 1989.

Utah: The Uniform Commercial Code is one of the uniform laws drafted by the National Conference of Commissioners on Uniform State Laws and the American Law Institute Governing Commercial Transactions. The purpose was to include laws relating to sales, leasing of goods, transfer of funds, commercial paper, bank deposits, collections, letters of credit, warehouse receipts, bills of lading, investment securities, and secured transactions. The Uniform Commercial Code was adopted under Title 70A.

Vermont: The Uniform Commercial Code is one of the uniform laws drafted by the National Conference of Commissioners on the Uniform State Laws and the American Law Institute Governing Commercial Transactions. (See *Black's Law Dictionary,* 1990 edition.) The Uniform Commercial Code was drafted to regulate sales, leasing of goods, transfer of funds, commercial paper, bank deposits, collections, letters of credit, warehouse receipts, bills of lading, investment securities, and secured transactions, etc. The Uniform Commercial Code in the state of Vermont became effective January 1, 1967.

Virginia: The Uniform Commercial Code is one of the uniform laws drafted by the National Conference of Commissioners on Uniform State Laws and the American Law Institute Governing Commercial Transactions. (See *Black's Law Dictionary,* 1990 edition.) The purpose of the enactment of the Uniform Commercial Code was to make common the transactions relating to sales, leasing of goods, transfer of funds, commercial paper, bank deposits, collections, letters of credit, warehouse receipts, bills of lading, investment securities, and secured transactions. In Virginia, the Uniform Commercial Code became effective on January 1, 1966. (See Section 8.1-101 et. seq. of the Code of Virginia.)

Washington: The Uniform Commercial Code is one of the uniform laws drafted by the National Conference of Commissioners on Uniform State Laws and the American Law Institute Governing Commercial Transactions. (See *Black's Law Dictionary*, 1990 edition.) The purpose of the Uniform Commercial Code was to standardize sales, leasing of goods, transfer of funds, commercial paper, bank deposits, collections, letters of credit, warehouse receipts, bills of lading, investment securities, and secured transactions.

The Uniform Commercial Code became effective in Washington on July 1, 1967. The code is known as Title 62A of the Revised Code of Washington.

West Virginia: The Uniform Commercial Code is one of the uniform laws drafted by the National Conference of Commissioners on the Uniform State Laws and the American Law Institute Governing Commercial Transactions. (See *Black's Law Dictionary*, 1990 edition.) The purpose of the Uniform Commercial Code was to make uniform various transactions involving sales, leasing of goods, transfer of funds, commercial paper, bank deposits, collections, letters of credit, warehouse receipts, bills of lading, investment securities, and secured transactions. The Commercial Code in West Virginia was enacted in its entirety and became effective July 1, 1964.

Wisconsin: The Uniform Commercial Code is one of the laws drafted by the National Conference of Commissioners on the Uniform State Laws and the American Law Institute Governing Commercial Transactions. (See *Black's Law Dictionary*, 1990 edition.) The purpose of the Uniform Commercial Code was to set forth common laws relating to sales, leasing of goods, transfer of funds, commercial paper, bank deposits, collections, letters of credit, warehouse receipts, bills of lading, investment securities, and secured transactions. The Uniform Commercial Code has been adopted and followed by the state of Wisconsin. For the Uniform Commercial Code, see Wisconsin Statute Section 401.101 et. seq.

Wyoming: The Uniform Commercial Code is one of the uniform laws drafted by the National Conference of Commissioners on the Uniform State Laws and the American Law Institute Governing Commercial Transactions. It was principally drafted for the purpose of establishing common laws relating to sales, leasing of goods, transfer of funds, commercial paper, bank deposits, collections, letters of credit, warehouse receipts, bills of lading, investment securities, and secured transactions. (See *Black's Law Dictionary*, 1990 edition.) In Wyoming, the Uniform Commercial Code became effective January 1, 1962, and is found under Chapter 34.

What is the consumer code?

Most states have a Consumer Code, which regulates fraud and deceptive business practices in the state. The act, in most states, is generally modeled after the Federal Trade Commission Act, and, in the process, certain unlawful practices regarding collection, sales, and representations are covered. Phone solicitation is generally covered, along with the giving of prizes, gifts, gratuities, auto and home repairs, etc. Conditions relating to loans, both as to real estate and non-real-estate items, are also protected under most state Consumer Codes.

Sample Forms

The sample forms in this chapter are completed with fictitious information in order to illustrate how the forms should be completed. Opposite each page of the sample form are end notes, which correspond to the filled-in information in the completed sample form. This chapter illustrates how to use the blank forms in Chapter 5. The chapters may be used together by matching the sample form (in Chapter 4) to the corresponding blank form in Chapter 5.

Sample Form
APARTMENT LEASE

THIS AGREEMENT, dated this <u>1st</u>[1] day of <u>June</u>[1], <u>1996</u>[1], by and between <u>Patrick Small</u>[2] of <u>330 First Street, Happy Willow, Ohio</u>[3], hereinafter referred to as tenant, and <u>Frank Bosworth</u>[4] of <u>111 Summit Avenue, St. Paul, Minnesota</u>[5], hereinafter referred to as landlord, recite the following terms and conditions:

1. **THE DESCRIPTION OF PREMISES:** Tenant hereby agrees to rent the premises described as follows:

<u>330 First Street, Happy Willow, Ohio</u>[6]

2. **TERM:** Tenant agrees to lease the above described premises for a period of <u>two(2)</u>[7] years commencing on the <u>1st</u>[8] day of <u>June</u>[8], <u>1996</u>[8], and ending on the <u>31st</u>[9] day of <u>May</u>[9], <u>1998</u>[9].

3. **RENTAL AMOUNT:** Tenant agrees to rent the aforementioned premises for the amount of <u>$495</u>[10] per month payable on the <u>1st</u>[11] day of each month after the <u>1st</u>[12] day of <u>June</u>[12], <u>1996</u>[12], the date of the first rental payment.

4. **SPECIAL CONDITIONS:** Tenant agrees to be bound by the special conditions for the premises as set out in the attached Rules and Regulations.

5. **CONDITION OF PREMISES:** Tenant agrees to maintain the premises in good condition at all times during possession and shall be certain that the premises are maintained in the condition as the premises were when first received by the tenant. In the event there are any problems with the premises which involve damage of any sort, the tenant must bring such matters to the immediate attention of the landlord.

6. **DAMAGE DEPOSIT:** Tenant agrees to place with the landlord a damage deposit equal to one month's rent, which amount is <u>$495</u>[13].

7. **SURRENDER OF PREMISES:** Tenant shall surrender the premises to Landlord immediately upon termination of this agreement.

8. **TERMINATION:** In the event tenant fails to perform any of the conditions of this Lease, the landlord shall have the option to provide notice to the tenant of tenant's failure to comply. Landlord shall have the rights of the three day notice to quit in the event of noncompliance with this agreement or in the event of nonpayment of rent in conjunction with this lease.

The form opposite is an example of how a typical form for the Apartment Lease may be completed. A blank version of this form (for your use) appears on pages 107–108.

1. This date reflects the date the document is signed between the parties.

2. The full name of the tenant.

3. The address of the tenant. Generally, this is the same address as that of the premises that the tenant rents from the landlord.

4. The full name of the landlord. Sometimes this is a corporation, in which case the agent of the corporation would sign at the bottom of the agreement.

5. The address of the landlord. Oftentimes, this is the same address as the address of the tenant, depending upon the facility that is rented.

6. The location of the premises is described in this space and, on occasion, this may be different from number 3 above. Sometimes the legal description may be required; however, often just the street address is sufficient.

7. Either the number of months or years for which the lease applies.

8. The day the lease agreement commences to run.

9. The day the lease terminates or ends.

10. The amount of rental per month.

11. The day of each month when the rental amount is due.

12. The day the first rental payment is due; most generally, this coincides with the first date of possession.

13. This is the amount of the damage deposit. Sometimes this is regulated by state statute or by city statute, such as in the case of New York.

Sample Form: Apartment Lease *(continued)*

9. <u>**USE:**</u> Tenant shall use the premises for <u>living purposes</u>[14] only and may not use the premise for any other purpose without the expressed written consent of landlord.

10. <u>**RIGHT TO ENTER:**</u> Landlord shall have the right to enter the premises at any reasonable time for the purpose of inspection.

11. <u>**APPLICABLE LAW:**</u> The law that governs this Agreement is the law of the State of <u>Ohio</u>[15]. In the event the landlord finds it necessary to enforce the provisions of this agreement against the tenant, the landlord shall be entitled to reasonable attorney's fees and costs. (<u>See Ohio Statutes</u>)[16].

12. <u>**ADDITIONAL PROVISIONS:**</u>

<u>No Pets Permitted</u>[17]

_____   _____

<u>TENANT</u>[18]   <u>LANDLORD</u>[19]

This is not a substitute for legal advice. An attorney must be consulted.

The form opposite is an example of how a typical form for the Apartment Lease may be completed.

14. The use of the premises should be described at this juncture.

15. The state under which the agreement may be enforced.

16. Although not necessary in most states, often a statute is cited.

17. Additional provisions are included in this space and, in this case, an example of no pets has been set forth.

18. Signature of the tenant.

19. Signature of the landlord.

Sample Form
TYPICAL APARTMENT RULES
AND REGULATIONS

1.) Tenant shall keep premises in good condition.

2.) Tenant shall not interfere with other tenant's premises.

3.) Tenant shall pay rent promptly on the due date.

4.) Tenant shall not make any alterations to the premises without written permission of the landlord.

5.) Tenant shall keep proper liability, fire and/or other damage insurance on the contents of the premises leased.

6.) Tenant shall not receive a refund of the damage deposit until landlord is certain that the premises are free of damages upon the surrender of the premises.

7.) No tenant shall interfere in any manner with any portion either of the heating or lighting or other apparatus in or about the building.

8.) Automobiles must be kept within yellow lines of the parking lot areas.

9.) Sanitary napkins shall not be deposited in toilets but shall be wrapped and deposited with other waste matter and refuse.

10.) Tenant shall be responsible for closing of windows in his or her apartment during storms.

11.) Doors to apartments shall be kept closed at all times.

12.) Owner shall have the right to inspect apartment at reasonable times.

13.) There shall be no door-to-door soliciting of any kind on said premises.

14.) Owner shall furnish extra keys and replace lost keys for $1.00 each. Upon the expiration of lease, tenant shall account for all keys delivered by owner.

15.) The landlord reserves the right: (1) to change any of the foregoing rules by rescinding or amending, or (2) to make such other rules or regulations as are deemed necessary to provide for the comfort and convenience of all tenants, and for the safety, care, proper maintenance and cleanliness of the premises.

16.) It is recommended that garbage disposal covers be kept in the drain position when the unit is not in use. This will prevent foreign material from dropping accidentally into the waste disposal unit. In using the equipment, be sure the cold water is turned on. It is important to maintain a sufficient flow of water to flush shredded waste, even after the disposal has been turned off. Please do not attempt to insert corn cobs, bottle caps, glass, pins, foil, crockery, rugs, string or paper into the disposal as this may cause malfunction and consequent inconvenience to you. Clogged disposal will be unclogged and/or repaired at the expense of the tenant.

The form opposite is an example of Apartment Rules and Regulations. A blank version of this form (for your use) appears on page 109–110.

No information needs to be added to this form.

Sample Form: Typical Apartment Rules and Regulations *(continued)*

17.) Laundry rooms are equipped with coin-operated washers and dryers. Kindly remove clothes promptly from machine. Do not use tints or dyes in the units. Please follow operating instructions and report any difficulty whatsoever.

18.) No doormats or other obstructions should be placed at your entrance door. Mail or paper deliveries should be taken in as soon as possible to minimize the possibility of accidents to passersby.

19.) Please advise owner promptly of any malfunctions or difficulties so that repairs and/or adjustments can be made at the least inconvenience to you.

20.) Nothing shall be attached to walls or woodwork except the stick-on type fasteners or small nails driven at an angle.

The form opposite is an example of Apartment Rules and Regulations.

No information needs to be added to this form.

Sample Form
BUSINESS LEASE AGREEMENT

This **LEASE AGREEMENT**, executed in duplicate, is made and entered into this 1st day of July, 1996[1], by and between Les Johnson Enterprises[2] of 12 Harding Road, Omaha, Nebraska[3], hereinafter called "LESSOR," and Sally Stiles[4] of 321 Parkway Avenue, Council Bluffs, Iowa[5], hereinafter called "LESSEE."

WITNESSETH

1. **PREMISES:** LESSOR, in consideration of the rents herein agreed to be paid and in conjunction with the agreements and conditions herein contained, does hereby demise and lease unto LESSEE the following described premises:

Premises to be leased for hair salon and barbershop[6].

2. **RENT:** LESSEE shall pay to LESSOR on the first day of each month from the 1st day of August, 1996[7], up to and including the 31st day of July, 2010[8], for the premises in paragraph one of this Lease, in the amount of $450.00[9] each month. Rent may be adjusted every year by the LESSOR and will be tied to the mortgage rate of a major lending institution.

3. **TERM:** The term of this lease shall be for a period of 14[10] years commencing on the 1st day of August, 1996[11], and shall end on the 31st day of July, 2010[12], or on such earlier date pursuant to this written agreement or this lease may be terminated pursuant to the conditions of this Lease or pursuant to law.

4. **USE:** The leased premises shall be used for hair salon and barbershop (storage and related purposes including, without limitation, administrative and sales offices)[13] for the conduct of the business of the LESSEE. LESSEE, agrees that leased premises shall not be used for any immoral or unlawful purposes, nor shall the premises be used for sleeping or living purposes, or in any manner that may tend to increase the risk of fire, other dangers or insurance rates.

5. **UTILITIES:** The LESSEE agrees to provide payment for all utilities. LESSOR shall not be liable for stoppage of any utility services including stoppages for needed repair or improvements or any cause beyond LESSOR's control.

The form opposite is an example of how a typical form for the Business Lease Agreement may be completed. A blank version of this form (for your use) appears on pages 111–115.

1. The date of the lease agreement was randomly selected.

2. A fictitious name has been inserted for the name of the Lessor.

3. A fictitious address for the leasing party or Lessor has been selected.

4. The name of the Lessee is to be included at this point.

5. The address of the Lessee.

6. A description of the purpose for the use of the premises should be included.

7. The day when the rental is due; this is the first date rental is due under the lease.

8. The last day for which the lease would be effective.

9. The amount of rental per month.

10. The period of duration for the lease.

11. The day the lease commences.

12. The day the lease terminates.

13. A description of the general use of the premises should be included at this juncture.

Sample Form: Business Lease Agreement *(continued)*

6. **LIABILITY FOR INJURY**[14]: LESSOR shall not be liable or responsible for any accident or injury to the person or property of LESSEE or anyone else that may arise from, or on, said premises. This provision shall apply to damage caused by water, snow, frost, steam, sewage, sewer gas or odors, bursting or leaking pipes, faucets and plumbing fixtures, and shall apply without distinction as to whose act nor neglect is responsible for the damage and whether the same was due to the specifically enumerated above or to some other cause of an entirely different kind. LESSEE is to hold LESSOR harmless for any damages to any person or persons caused by or resulting in any way from LESSEE's negligence or that of any person in LESSEE's employ or any persons on said premises by the permission or invitation of LESSEE. LESSEE should have no claim for damages resulting from any defect in the leased premises, unless the LESSOR shall have failed to remedy such defect within reasonable time after receiving written notice from the LESSEE of its existence.

7. **FIRE INSURANCE AND WAIVER OF SUBROGATION**[15]: LESSOR shall cause each insurance policy carried by LESSOR to include protection for the demised premises against loss by fire and other causes covered by standard extended coverage, and LESSEE shall do the same. Such insurance shall be written in a manner so as to provide that the insurance carrier waives all right of recovery by way of subrogation against LESSOR or LESSEE in connection with any loss or damage covered by any such policies. Neither party shall be liable to the other for any loss or damage caused by fire or any of the risks enumerated in standard extended coverage insurance. However, if such waiver cannot be obtained or is obtainable only by the payment of an additional premium, the party undertaking such insurance coverage shall have a period of ten(10) days after the giving of such notice either to: (a) place such insurance in companies which are reasonably satisfactory to the other party and will carry such insurance with wavier of subrogation, or (b) agree to pay such additional premium if such policy is obtainable at additional cost. If the release of either the LESSOR or LESSEE as set forth in the second sentence of this paragraph shall contravene any law with respect to exculpatory agreements, the liability of the LESSOR or LESSEE, as the case may be, shall be deemed not released but shall be deemed secondary to that of the insurer.

8. **ALTERATIONS:** The premises shall not be altered or changed without written consent of the LESSOR, and all alterations or improvements or additions desired by the LESSEE and to which LESSOR has agreed shall be made under the direction of the LESSOR but at the expense of the LESSEE. All improvements, alterations or additions

The form opposite is an example of how a typical form for the Business Lease Agreement may be completed.

14. Liability for injury and insurance coverage relating to same may vary from state to state and may vary between the agreement of the parties. An attorney should be consulted regarding this particular feature.

15. Fire insurance and waiver of subrogation will vary between states; however, the language that is included here is intended to be fairly standard and should apply in most states. An attorney should be consulted.

Sample Form: Business Lease Agreement *(continued)*

(except LESSEE's moveable furniture and barber equipment[16]) shall, in the absence of written agreement to the contrary, remain on and be surrendered with the premises at the expiration of the term of this lease by lapse of time or otherwise.

9. **MAINTENANCE AND REPAIRS:** LESSEE shall make all repairs to the demised premises including, but not limited to: plumbing, heating, electrical and air conditioning equipment repairs.

10. **ABATEMENT**[17]**:** LESSEE shall not be entitled to compensation or abatement of rent because of any inconvenience or annoyance arising from the making of repairs or the alteration to the building, or from any work done at the building, or other operations conducted on structures erected on any adjacent building or the premises, or because of interference with view, light, air or wire by reason thereof.

11. **RENT IN CASE OF CASUALTY**[18]**:** If the premises be rendered untenable by fire, wind, storm, or other cause, no rent shall accrue until the premises are again ready for occupancy providing any such damage shall not be the fault or negligence of the LESSEE or LESSEE's employees or licensees. In case the premises are not restored to tenantable condition within one hundred twenty(120) days[19] after such casualty, either party may terminate this lease and the rent shall be apportioned and paid to the time that the premises became untenable.

12. **ASSIGNMENT**[20]**:** This lease may not be assigned, nor any part of the leased premises sublet to anyone without the LESSOR's expressed written consent. No extension or alteration of this lease shall be binding unless the same is in writing and signed by both parties hereto.

13. **WAIVER:** Waiver of any portion of any of the provisions of this lease shall not constitute a waiver of any other portion.

14. **HOLDING OVER:** If the LESSOR, without executing a new written lease shall allow the LESSEE to remain in possession of the premises after the expiration of this lease, the LESSEE shall become a tenant from month-to-month, under the same conditions of this lease except as to the duration. Any such tenancy may be terminated through the transmittal of thirty(30)[21] days' written notice by either party.

15. **SURRENDER:** Upon the expiration or any earlier termination of this lease, LESSEE shall surrender the leased premises to LESSOR in the good order and condition as received upon the date of the commencement of this lease, reasonable wear and tear excepted.

The form opposite is an example of how a typical form for the Business Lease Agreement may be completed.

16. Exceptions to the alterations, improvements, and additions should be placed in this particular blank. It should be noted that this is tailor-made for the hypothetical lease that has been drafted.

17. In regard to abatement, this may vary from state to state. An attorney should be consulted.

18. Arbitrary language has been used regarding rent in the case of casualty; however, this may vary from state to state. An attorney should be consulted.

19. A period of 120 days was selected as an example. A reasonable period of time is generally noted and may be subject to local or state laws.

20. Assignment of leases is generally liberally construed in favor of the Lessee, providing that the subletting of premises is done for reasonable purpose and providing further that the landlord/Lessor is provided appropriate notification in advance. There may be special restrictions in given states or cities; therefore, an attorney should be consulted.

21. An arbitrary date of 30 days has been selected. This would vary from state to state.

Sample Form: Business Lease Agreement *(continued)*

16. **INTEREST ON UNPAID SUMS:** LESSEE agrees that any and all sums due hereunder and unpaid when due shall draw interest after the due date at the rate of <u>ten percent(10%)</u>[22] per annum, and that all sums unpaid by the <u>30th</u>[23] day of each month shall be adjusted to include a <u>ten percent(10%)</u>[24] penalty.

17. **LIEN DUE TO UNPAID SUMS**[25]**:** LESSEE hereby agrees that the rent and/or rental penalties, whether due or to become due shall be a lien on any or all furniture and other property had or used on said premises at any time during the LESSEE's occupancy of the premises. It is mutually agreed that if any of the rent herein specified shall not be paid when due, or if there is a breach of any covenants contained in this agreement, it shall be optional with the LESSOR, at any time, to declare this lease void, and upon giving LESSEE three(3) days' Notice to Quit, as provided by law, to reenter said premises and remove all persons under an appropriate remedy under law including forcible entry or detinue. It is agreed that, in the event suit is commenced to collect rent or any part thereof, or to enforce any provision of this lease, or if suit is brought either by or against the LESSOR for any cause resulting from this lease, reasonable attorney fees shall be paid in addition to all other costs.

18. **PROPERTY AND MERCHANDISE:** LESSEE agrees that all property, goods or merchandise brought, deposited, stored or permitted by LESSEE to be present upon the premises shall be present at the exclusive liability and risk of the LESSEE.

19. **FIXTURES:** LESSEE agrees to repair or replace as applicable, all doors, windows, plumbing, gas, electric, steam or other fixtures broken or otherwise damaged on said premises during the use and tenancy by LESSEE.

20. **QUIET AND ENJOYMENT:** LESSOR represents and warrants to LESSEE that LESSOR has title in fee simple to the leased premises and that so long as LESSEE is paying rent and observing the covenants of this lease, the LESSEE shall quietly hold and enjoy the leased premises in the terms hereof.

21. **COMPLIANCE WITH LAWS:** LESSOR further represents and warrants that the building in which the leased premises are located, and the parking area, comply with applicable zoning and building regulations and that the LESSEE's use thereof in accordance with the provisions of this lease is permitted by such regulations.

22. **ADDITIONAL RULES:** The LESSOR reserves the right, when conditions warrant, to make additional rules governing LESSEE and its employees relating to the proper care of the building and preservation of good order.

23. **MODIFICATION OF LEASE:** The terms, covenants and conditions hereof may not be changed orally but only by an agreement in writing signed by the parties.

The form opposite is an example of how a typical form for the Business Lease Agreement may be completed.

22. The rate of ten percent per annum has been selected. This is generally permitted by specific agreement between the parties or another percentage may be used that does not violate the state usury laws. A form of percentage should be included. An attorney should be consulted as to appropriate rates that may be charged.

23. An arbitrary date was selected for the date of adjustments after which a penalty may occur.

24. An arbitrary figure of ten percent for penalty was inserted. This may vary from state to state. An attorney should be consulted.

25. Liens vary from state to state and an appropriate Notice to Quit may vary as to its time period from state to state. Therefore, an attorney should be consulted regarding any liens on unpaid sums and any appropriate Notice to Quit.

Sample Form: Business Lease Agreement *(continued)*

24. **SUCCESSOR AND ASSIGNS:** The terms, covenants and conditions of this lease shall be binding upon and shall inure to the benefit of LESSOR and LESSEE and their respective executors, administrators, heirs, distributees, legal representatives, successor and assigns.

25. **PARAGRAPH HEADING:** The paragraph headings herein contained are inserted only as a matter of convenience and for reference and, in no way, define, limit or describe the scope or intent of the lease or, in any way, affect the terms and provisions hereof.

26. **INSPECTION:** It is herein acknowledged that LESSEE has inspected the premises and accepts them in good order.

27. **OPTION TO RENEW:** Upon satisfaction of this initial duration lease ending on the 31st day of July, 2010[26], LESSEE is granted an option to renew for an additional ten(10)[27] year period under the same terms and conditions. The exercise of this option requires that LESSEE furnish LESSOR with written notice of intent to renew no less than sixty(60) days[28] prior to renewal date.

28. **ADDITIONAL PROVISIONS**[29]**:**

IN WITNESS WHEREOF, the parties hereto duly executed this lease in duplicate the day and year first above written.

_____

Owner of Premises[30]
First Party-Lessor

_____

Second Party-Lessee[32]

_____

Co-owner of Premises[31]
First Party-Lessor

_____NONE_____

Second Party-Co-Lessee[33]

The form opposite is an example of how a typical form for the Business Lease Agreement may be completed.

26. The concluding date of the lease is noted.

27. If an additional option is provided or sought, this would be the appropriate vehicle. An arbitrary date of ten years was selected.

28. The period of sixty days was randomly selected. Usually, this time period is left to the parties; however, some states or local governments may have minimum requirements.

29. The "Additional Provisions" section is left blank for this example. This section allows the parties to tailor-make additional requirements subject to state law for their own mutual agreement. It is also suggested that the particular state under which a lease shall be enforced should be stated. This boilerplate lease does not include that information; however, that information is important because this lease may be subject to either Nebraska or Iowa law depending upon the intent of the parties since both Omaha and Council Bluffs are the hypothetical cities used.

30. The owner of the premises or the owner's designated assignee.

31. A blank has been allowed for co-owner of the premises. In this case, we have shown the signature of the spouse of the owner.

32. The Lessee's signature. It should be noted that in some states, a verification by a Notary Public may be necessary in order for the lease to be appropriately filed with the government agency, such as the County Recorder or the Secretary of State, if need be. Also, in many states a verification by a Notary Public may be necessary if the lease term is longer than a specified period, such as one year.

33. There was an absence of a Co-Lessee in this case, so the word "none" has been entered. In many cases there is a Co-Lessee. For that reason, a signature space has been provided.

Sample Form
FARM LEASE AGREEMENT

THIS AGREEMENT, dated this <u>1st day of March, 1996</u>[1], by and <u>between Ole Johannson Farm Corporation</u>[2] of <u>3624 Dew Street, Minneapolis, Minnesota</u>[3], hereinafter referred to as the FIRST PARTY and <u>Fred Farmington</u>[4] of <u>RFD Owatona, Minnesota</u>[5], hereinafter referred to as SECOND PARTY, recite the following terms and conditions:

1. **LEASED PREMISES:** The FIRST PARTY in conjunction with the conditions contained herein does lease to the SECOND PARTY the following described real estate which is located in <u>Hennepin</u>[6] County, <u>State of Minnesota</u>[7]:

<u>160 Acres, more or less, legally described as:</u>

<u>The Northwest Quarter of Section 86, Township 4, Range 6</u>[8].

2. **LEASE PERIOD:** This lease shall commence on the <u>1st day of April, 1996</u>[9], and shall continue for <u>2</u>[10] year(s), approximately, ending on the <u>31st day of December, 1997</u>[11]. If this agreement is not terminated by either party in conjunction with the terms and conditions contained herein, it will automatically be renewed under the same terms and conditions for a period of one year, and if the lease is not renewed at the end of that year, it shall continue on a year-to-year basis under the same terms and conditions, providing same is not terminated or modified by the parties in writing.

3. **RENTAL TERMS**[12]**:** The SECOND PARTY agrees to pay the FIRST PARTY as rent for the above described real estate at the address of the FIRST PARTY, according to the following:

    A. The sum of $9,200 on April 1, 1996;

    B. The sum of $10,000 on November 1, 1996;

    C. The sum of $9,200 on the April 1, 1997; and

    D. The sum of $10,000 on November 1, 1997.

4. **CROP PRESENTATION:** The SECOND PARTY shall prepare annually a crop plan and shall present same to the FIRST PARTY on or before the first day of February of each year during the terms of this agreement. The crop plan shall provide a rationale for crop rotation, soil preservation and conservation, the means by which tilling will occur; a soil erosion control plan which includes maintenance of water courses, waterways, ditches, drainage areas, tiles, etc; and a method of crop production which allows for proper crop rotation during various crop seasons. The SECOND PARTY shall also annually provide a

The form opposite is an example of how a typical form for the Farm Lease Agreement may be completed. A blank version of this form (for your use) appears on pages 117–121.

1. The date the agreement is signed is first noted in this series of blanks.

2. The name of the landlord is included and should reflect the same name as the landlord uses to sign his signature.

3. The address of the landlord.

4. The name of the lessee as signed.

5. The address of the lessee.

6. The county in which the property is located.

7. The state in which the property is located.

8. Inserted is the legal description. The one enclosed is a fictitious description.

9. The date the lease commenced.

10. The number of years for which the lease runs. In this case it is approximately 2 years since the lease does not quite run for 2 years, which is often common for farm land.

11. The ending day of the lease.

12. The method of payment in this particular case is set out. It should be noted that the owner of the premises was desirous of approximately one-half of the funds in advance of the use of the ground and the other one-half to be paid in the fall of the year, presumably once the crop is harvested by the tenant.

Sample Form: Farm Lease Agreement *(continued)*

presentation as to the manner in which all crops will be harvested, cultivated and fertilized. Any use of commercial fertilizer, pesticides, insecticides and use of mineral additives to the soil will need to be included in the crop program annually by the SECOND PARTY for the review and approval of the FIRST PARTY. Any use of potash, phosphate, urea, dap, lime and other trace materials shall be included in an allocation plan during the term of the lease and a proposal by the SECOND PARTY to the FIRST PARTY and shall include a proposal relative to the payment of any minerals, etc. In the event the SECOND PARTY fails to perform in conjunction with the terms of this agreement or in conjunction with the crop presentation plan, as noted above, the FIRST PARTY reserves the right to enter the premises and allow for the proper care and harvest of all crops with appropriate costs for such care and harvest to the SECOND PARTY.

5. **PREMISES CONDITION:** Tenant shall always maintain the best practices relative to the condition of the premises including all land and buildings, fences, roads, tile, wells, lagoon and other facilities which are a part of the premises[13]. The SECOND PARTY shall assure that the above leased premises is maintained in good order and good condition. The premises must always be in substantially the same condition as received by the SECOND PARTY from the FIRST PARTY at the time this lease commenced.

6. **MACHINERY USE AND EQUIPMENT USE:** The cost of all machinery and equipment usage on the premises shall be at the expense of the SECOND PARTY, and such expense shall include the costs of all combining, shelling, harvesting, bailing and/or otherwise acquisition of crops from the premises. The maintenance and cost of the machinery, including all and any repairs, shall be paid by the SECOND PARTY. The SECOND PARTY, however, shall be permitted to use all buildings on the premises for storage of equipment and machinery with the exception of the following:

14

7. **SITE CARE:** The care of all buildings, roadways, trees, shrubs, grass, utility lines and other features placed upon the above described real estate shall be preserved and provided appropriate care by the SECOND PARTY; however, the application of paint, carpentry items and other repairs shall be paid by the FIRST PARTY on receipt of notice from the SECOND PARTY. Any such needs for repairs such as carpentry and/or paint, etc. should be paid by the FIRST PARTY after appropriate notice from the SECOND PARTY and after approval by the FIRST PARTY.

The form opposite is an example of how a typical form for the Farm Lease Agreement may be completed.

13. There are various government regulations that relate to wells, lagoons, and other use of property that may affect the environment and the property.

14. In the event there are exceptions to the use of the premises, such use should be noted.

Sample Form: Farm Lease Agreement *(continued)*

8. **TERMINATION**[15]**:** As provided in the provision relative to term noted above, the period of this agreement is for approximately 2[16] year(s). It may be renewed, if not terminated by either of the parties, for an additional 2 years approximately[17] if a new written lease agreement is not signed between the parties. This agreement shall automatically become null and void if the parties prepare an agreement to supersede this document or if the FIRST PARTY terminates this agreement for the failure of the SECOND PARTY to comply with any of its provisions. Notice of any failure to comply shall be provided by the FIRST PARTY to the SECOND PARTY immediately upon learning of non-compliance, and the SECOND PARTY shall have 10[18] days in which to respond and rectify the agreement breach. If a response is not satisfactory or timely made to the FIRST PARTY by the SECOND PARTY, the FIRST PARTY, at the option of the FIRST PARTY, may terminate this agreement.

9. **RIGHT OF INSPECTION:** At any time within reason, the FIRST PARTY may enter on the premises, within reason, for the purpose of viewing the SECOND PARTY'S use of the premises in compliance with this agreement. Once a Notice of Termination of this agreement has been provided to the SECOND PARTY, the FIRST PARTY reserves the right to enter upon the premises for the purpose of farming, planting and harvesting the crops on the premises.

10. **REMEDIES:** If either of the parties violates the terms of this agreement, the other shall have all rights permitted by law to pursue legal and equitable remedies to which the party is entitled. A failure by the SECOND PARTY to pay any rent when due shall be grounds for the termination of this agreement and shall immediately cause all unpaid rent to be due and owing without any additional notice by the FIRST PARTY to the SECOND PARTY. All remedies accorded shall be pursuant to Minnesota[19] law and shall include appropriate state statutes[20].

11. **SHARECROP:** In the event the parties have agreed that a rental shall be pursuant to a form of share in the crop raised on the premises, all product raised on the premises shall be harvested and located at the specific location to which the parties agree and, in every event, the FIRST PARTY consents. The terms of the sharecrop and the percentage to each party shall be attached hereto as Attachment "A[21]."

12. **LANDLORD LIEN**[22]**:** The FIRST PARTY shall have a lien on all the SECOND PARTY's personal property located on the above described real estate and shall have a lien on all crops raised on the premises (growing or grown) until such time the payments due for rental by the SECOND PARTY to the FIRST PARTY are made. The SECOND PARTY shall provide a list of the crops grown and sign appropriate financing statements in order to allow

The form opposite is an example of how a typical form for the Farm Lease Agreement may be completed.

15. Termination may vary from state to state. In this regard, an attorney must be consulted.

16. It should be noted that this lease is for approximately 2 years. This is an arbitrary figure chosen for this example.

17. This is an allowance for renewal of the lease.

18. A ten-day period was allowed by virtue of the sample contract to permit the tenant to rectify any breach. This may be a very short period of time and, in some states, it may require a more lengthy period.

19. The name of the state is reflected.

20. A particular state statute may be inserted at this juncture.

21. If there is a sharecrop arrangement, an Attachment A should be made a part of the agreement. It should be noted that in this particular case there is not a sharecrop arrangement pursuant to the rental agreement under paragraph 3; therefore, it is not necessary for there to be an Attachment A. In such cases, an attorney should be consulted. If there is not a sharecrop arrangement, the non-applicable part of the contract should be deleted.

22. In most states, a landlord is permitted a lien on crops growing or grown to assure payment of appropriate rent. The various states allow for agricultural liens under different circumstances; therefore, an attorney should be consulted.

Sample Form: Farm Lease Agreement *(continued)*

the FIRST PARTY to protect appropriate liens and security interests so that the FIRST PARTY has a first lien and security interest on the crops grown in order to protect the rental due to the FIRST PARTY.

13. **IMPROVEMENTS**[23]**:** Any buildings, fences or improvements of any kind made by the SECOND PARTY upon the premises during the term of the agreement shall constitute additional rent and shall ensure to the benefit of the real estate and be the property of the FIRST PARTY. No expenses for the improvement of the premises shall be incurred without the expressed permission of the FIRST PARTY except that the SECOND PARTY agrees to maintain, at his cost, all well and other water sewage systems on the premises except in the event of damage caused by natural catastrophe.

14. **GOVERNMENT PROGRAMS:** The participation in any government programs provided by the United States Department of Agriculture for the state of Minnesota shall be exclusively at the option of the FIRST PARTY. Payments from participation in such programs shall be divided between the FIRST PARTY and the SECOND PARTY as agreed between them in writing. Such agreement shall be attached hereto as Attachment "B[24]."

15. **NOTICES**[25]**:** All notices contemplated under this lease shall be made in writing, delivered in person or mailed in the United States mail, return receipt requested to the last known address of the recipient.

16. **POSSESSION:** The SECOND PARTY shall receive possession of the premises on the 1st day of April, 1996[26] and shall have the premises subject to the terms and conditions of this lease until the 31st day of December, 1997[27]. In the event of termination of this lease for any reason, the premises shall be relinquished to the possession of the FIRST PARTY.

17. **WRITTEN CHANGES:** Any changes to this agreement must be made in writing and executed by both parties in an addendum to this agreement.

18. **ACCOUNTING:** The method used for dividing and accounting of any harvest of grain, if applicable, shall be performed in the following manner:

Accounting shall not be necessary so long as the tenant
is in compliance with paragraph 3 in this agreement.[28]

19. **APPLICABLE LAW:** The laws of the State of Minnesota[29] shall apply to this agreement. If either party is compelled to enforce the terms of this agreement, the prevailing party shall be entitled to recover reasonable attorney's fees and costs.

The form opposite is an example of how a typical form for the Farm Lease Agreement may be completed.

23. Improvements may be governed or regulated under specific terminology by virtue of state statutes. Therefore, state statutes should be reviewed in the presence of an attorney.

24. Oftentimes, agricultural land may be subject to government programs which are provided by the United States Department of Agriculture. The participation in government programs may allow for certain payments for which the state should be identified and a special attachment should be set forth if the attachment and agreement are going to relate to the method of rental payment or compensation.

25. Notices may vary from state to state. In this particular case, the ordinary mail is used as the means for notice.

26. The 1st day of April, 1996, was used as the first date of possession.

27. The 31st day of December, 1997, was the last date of possession and was arbitrarily selected for demonstration purposes.

28. Many times a specific method of accounting may be required if there involves sharecropping and/or government programs or other unique features to the Farm Lease Agreement. An attorney should be consulted.

29. The state of Minnesota was arbitrarily selected for this particular lease, and the Minnesota statutes would apply.

Sample Form: Farm Lease Agreement *(continued)*

20. __ADDITIONAL PROVISIONS__[30]:

Dated on this <u>1st day of March, 1996</u>[31] at <u>Minneapolis, Minnesota</u>[32].

_____   _____
<u>Owner of Premises/First Party</u>[33]   <u>Leasing Party/Second Party</u>[34]

STATE OF <u>MINNESOTA</u>[35])
)
COUNTY OF <u>HENNEPIN</u>[36])

On this <u>1st day of March, 1996</u>[37], before me, the undersigned Notary Public in and for <u>Hennepin</u>[38] County and the State of Minnesota, personally appeared the individuals who are identified above as the First Party and the Second Party who acknowledged to me to be the persons who are named in the agreement and who executed the foregoing agreement as their voluntary act and deed.

_____
<u>NOTARY PUBLIC</u>[39]

The form opposite is an example of how a typical form for the Farm Lease Agreement may be completed.

30. A blank has been provided for additional provisions which the parties may wish to have in their agreement.

31. The date the agreement is signed has been noted.

32. The place the agreement was signed has been noted.

33. The full signature of the owner of the premises.

34. The full signature of the leasing party.

35. The state where the document was executed.

36. The county where the document was executed.

37. The date the document was executed before a Notary Public.

38. The county in which the document was executed before a Notary Public.

39. Signature of the Notary Public.

Sample Form
PROMISSORY NOTE
(LONG FORM)

DEBTOR: <u>Richard Aldebt, 121 Small Street</u>[1]

CREDITOR: <u>Last National Bank, 293 Highway 5</u>[2]

DATE OF NOTE: <u>May 1, 1996</u>[3]

AMOUNT OF NOTE: <u>$100,000</u>[4]

INTEREST RATE: <u>8%</u>[5]

PURPOSE OF NOTE: <u>Working Capital</u>[6]

MATURITY DATE: <u>April 30, 1997</u>[7]

1. **PROMISE:** ON THIS <u>1st day of April, 1996</u>[8], the undersigned first party (debtor) jointly and severally agree as principals to pay the second party (creditor), its successors, agents and/or assigns the amount of <u>$100,000</u>[9] (principal amount) plus interest in the amount of <u>8%</u>[10] (rate of interest).

2. **PAYMENT:** The payment of the above noted amount plus interest at the above identified rate shall be paid either: (a) in a <u>single payment</u>[11] in the amount of <u>$108,000</u>[12] (total amount of principal plus total amount of interest) on the maturity date of the <u>30th day of April, 1997</u>[7]; or (b) in (number of installments) installments of $_____ on the ____ day of each month after the date of this note until fully paid and, in no event, shall final payment of principal and interest extend beyond the maturity date of this note, the <u>30th day of April, 1997</u>[13]. Interest shall be first deducted from the payment made, with the balance of the payment applied to the principal.

3. **INTEREST:** The interest of the principal amount due on this note is <u>8%</u>[14] per annum. If the interest and principal is not paid when due, the unpaid balance shall draw a higher rate of interest of <u>9-1/2%</u>[15] per annum.

4. **SECURITY:** Any security offered in conjunction with this note is identified as: <u>accounts receivables</u>[16](description of property offered as security). An appropriate UCC form may be filed with the proper authority including the Secretary of State or County Recorder in conjunction with any security interest held in conjunction with this paragraph.

5. **CONSUMER CREDIT:** This agreement is not considered by the parties to be a consumer credit transaction. This transaction is subject to the Uniform Commercial Code of the State of <u>Illinois</u>[17].

6. **DEFAULT**[18]**:** This note shall be considered to be in default whenever there exists: (a) failure to pay either interest or principal when same is due; (b) death of the debtor; (c) failure by the debtor to comply with any provisions of this agreement including the pledging

The form opposite is an example of how a typical form for the Promissory Note (Long) may be completed. A blank version of this form (for your use) appears on pages 123–125.

1. The full name and address of the party who owes the debt should be included here.

2. The full name and address of the bank or party to whom the debt is owed.

3. The date of the note or the date the debt is incurred is noted at this space.

4. The total amount borrowed should be inserted at this point.

5. The rate of interest needs to be disclosed at this point.

6. The use for which the money is being loaned should be set forth.

7. The date the note is due should be stated.

8. The date the note is signed.

9. The total amount of the note.

10. The rate of interest should be set forth.

11. Two options are provided in this sample note: (1) the option of a single payment, which includes the amount of the note, plus interest, or (2) the option of installments, which is subparagraph (b). In this particular case, the option of single payment was chosen and has been completed for illustration purposes.

12. The total amount of the principal, plus the amount of interest, is shown.

13. The maturity date when the principal and interest are due is set forth.

14. The amount of interest for the note is set forth. This may be regulated by state law; therefore, it is important to consult legal counsel as to the rates that may be charged.

15. A higher rate of interest may be charged if the note is not paid on a timely basis. Again, an attorney should be consulted.

16. In this particular case, the security offered happens to be accounts receivable. Other security may be offered including real estate or personal property, etc., subject to state law.

17. The state in which the transaction is regulated should be set forth.

18. Various bases for default are set forth under this paragraph 6. These may vary from state to state; therefore, an attorney should be consulted.

Sample Form: Promissory Note (Long Form) *(continued)*

of items listed as security in this agreement to any other party; (d) insolvency or business failure by the debtor; (e) any assignments for the benefits of other creditors or the filing of bankruptcy by the debtor; (f) any attachments, liens or acquisitions which, in any way, affect property offered in this agreement as security or collateral; (g) any untrue statements, misrepresentations or misstatements made by debtor; or (h) any occurrence of default or breach of any agreements by debtor which may relate to this note or the security offered.

7. **REMEDIES**[19]**:** In the event of default, all amounts of principal and interest are deemed due and owing to the second party. The second party creditor to this agreement shall be entitled to all remedies permitted by law. Additionally, the second party shall be entitled to recover all expenses related to collection including attorney fees and costs from the first party, if collection is necessary. Such amounts shall be in addition to any interest, penalty interest, and principal amounts due.

8. **LAW APPLICABLE:** The law of the State of <u>Illinois</u>[20] shall apply to this agreement. Failure at any time to exercise certain options available to the second party under this control shall not be deemed a waiver of any rights provided under Illinois law on this agreement by the second party. The second party may exercise its rights and options under this agreement at a time later than the date when any sums may come due and the second party may make demand for payment at any time after such payments fall due.

9. **INSPECTION:** The second party may inspect, copy and review the first party's books and records at any reasonable time.

10. **ASSIGNMENT OR SALE**[21]**:** The second party may assign or sell its interest in this agreement at any time and without notice to the first party.

11. **OTHER PROVISIONS:**

Dated at <u>Chicago, Illinois</u>[22] (location where note is signed) on this <u>1st day of April, 1996</u>[23].

_____   _____

Signature of Second[24]   Signature of First[25]
Party/Creditor   Party/Debtor

_____   _____

Address of Second Party[26]   Address of First Party[27]

This is not a substitute for legal advice. An attorney must be consulted.

The form opposite is an example of how a typical form for the Promissory Note (Long) may be completed.

19. The remedies to which the parties have agreed are set forth and again this matter is something that may change subject to state regulations. Therefore, an attorney must be consulted.

20. The state of Illinois has been chosen as the state applicable, since the note was written in Illinois.

21. It is possible under certain circumstances and in certain states for the notes to be assigned. Many times banks will assign notes to other parties, and that designation has been set forth in this agreement. Again, an attorney should be consulted relative to this particular language.

22. The location of Chicago, Illinois, was arbitrarily selected.

23. The date on which the note was signed should be set forth.

24. The signature of the authorized agent of the Second Party Creditor.

25. The signature of the First Party Debtor.

26. The address of the Second Party/Creditor.

27. The address of the First Party/Debtor.

Sample Form
PROMISSORY NOTE
(SHORT FORM)

The undersigned <u>Ron Leonard</u>[1] (debtor or first party) of <u>8338 San Elena Dr., Los Angeles, California</u>[2], (first party's address) hereby agrees to pay the sum of <u>$6,000</u>[3] to <u>Robert Loxly</u>[4], (creditor or second party) of <u>667 Pacific Coast Parkway, San Diego, California</u>[5], (second party's address) plus interest from the <u>1st day of June, 1996</u>[6], at the rate of <u>10%</u>[7] per annum in consideration of: (here state the reason such as money loaned, etc.) Repayment shall be made according to the following <u>schedule</u>[8]:

<u>July 1, 1996</u>	-	<u>$2,000</u>(amount of payment)[8]
<u>August 1, 1996</u>	-	<u>$2,000</u>(amount of payment)
<u>September 1, 1996</u>	-	<u>$2,000</u>(amount of payment)

Interest due at the time of payment shall be deducted first; then the remainder of the payment shall be applied to principal. Upon failure to pay when due, <u>Ron Leonard</u>[9] (first party) shall be immediately obligated to pay the full amount of principal, all interest plus costs and attorney fees, if any, incurred for recovery by <u>Robert Loxly</u>[10] (second Party).

This Note is subject to the laws of the State of <u>California</u>[11].

Dated this <u>1st day of June, 1996</u>[12], at <u>Los Angeles, California</u>[13] (location where note is signed).

_____

Witness Signature[14]

_____

Signature of Debtor/First Party[15]

_____

Address of Debtor/First Party[16]

The form opposite is an example of how a typical form for the Promissory Note (Short) may be completed. A blank version of this form (for your use) appears on page 127.

1. An arbitrary name for the debtor party has been selected. Generally, the short form promissory note is used for minimal amounts of sums that are borrowed. Usually, the short form promissory note is used between individuals who know each other and acknowledge a short-term loan for repayment within a fairly short period of time.

2. The address of the debtor should be set forth.

3. The principal sum of the note.

4. The name of the creditor or second party to whom the note is given for the sums received.

5. The address of the party who loaned the sums to the debtor.

6. The date from which interest should run. Often, this is the same date the document is signed.

7. The rate of interest that is charged should be set forth. This is regulated by state statute and, for that reason, an attorney should be consulted.

8. A repayment schedule is set forth.

9. The name of the party borrowing is set forth.

10. The name of the party loaning the funds is set forth.

11. The state under which the laws apply to the document is set forth. Many times variations of this agreement will exist from state to state; therefore, this document must be reviewed by an attorney.

12. The date on which the document was signed.

13. The location where the document was signed.

14. The signature of a witness should be placed at this juncture. However, many times verification or, in other words, signature before a Notary Public may be necessary before the promissory note may be valid. Therefore, an attorney should be consulted.

15. The signature of the debtor.

16. The address of the debtor.

Sample Form
SECURITY AGREEMENT

Debtor   Richard Aldebt[1]

Address of Debtor   121 Small Street, Chicago, Illinois[2]

Creditor   Last National Bank[3]

Address of Creditor   293 Highway 5, Chicago, Illinois[4]

THIS AGREEMENT, made between the undersigned DEBTOR, Richard Aldebt[5] (name of debtor) of 121 Small Street, Chicago, Illinois[6] (address of debtor), and the undersigned CREDITOR, Last National Bank[7] (name of creditor) of 293 Highway 5, Chicago, Illinois[8] (address of creditor), is entered in conjunction with the following:

1. **PROPERTY:** The property the undersigned DEBTOR is providing as collateral to the CREDITOR is described as follows:

   Accounts receivable and entire inventory for debtor's tire
   sales and service company[9].

2. **INDEBTEDNESS:** The debt for which the above noted collateral is offered as security is a result from the debt occurred by the DEBTOR to the CREDITOR as described as follows:

   Line of credit to acquire inventory for tire sales business.
   The full expected costs of $100,000[10].

3. **PURPOSE:** The reason for this security interest in the above described property as collateral is to:

   To continue operations of existing tire store[11].

4. **DEFAULT**[12]**:** In the event of default in failure to pay by the DEBTOR to the CREDITOR the amounts due and owing to the CREDITOR pursuant to an agreement evidencing any obligations to the CREDITOR, the result shall be the CREDITOR declaring the

The form opposite is an example of how a typical form for the Security Agreement may be completed. A blank version of this form (for your use) appears on pages 129–130.

1. The identity of the debtor.

2. The address of the debtor.

3. The identity of the creditor.

4. The address of the creditor.

5. The name of the debtor.

6. The address of the debtor.

7. The name of the creditor. This may also include the agent for the creditor.

8. The address of the creditor.

9. The property that is offered as collateral.

10. The description of the debt.

11. The reason for the security interest. Oftentimes, this will be very similar to 10 above.

12. Default may be regulated by state statutes; therefore, an attorney must be consulted.

Sample Form: Security Agreement *(continued)*

obligations immediately due and payable. The CREDITOR shall have all remedies according to a secured party under the Uniform Commercial Code of Illinois[13].

     5. **FILING**[14]**:** The CREDITOR (secured party), at his option, may file this security agreement with the Secretary of State or the appropriate County Recorder or both.

     6. **ADDITIONAL PROVISIONS**[15]**:**

None

_____   _____

DEBTOR[16]   CREDITOR[17]

STATE OF ILLINOIS[18]   )
)ss
COUNTY OF COOK[19]   )

     On this 1st day of May, 1996[20], the persons identified above, Richard Aldebt and David Vanderbilt, III, agent,[21](list parties) signed before me, a Notary Public, their signatures when they personally appeared to declare the above voluntary act and deed.

_____

NOTARY PUBLIC[22]

The form opposite is an example of how a typical form for the Security Agreement may be completed.

13. The state in which the Commercial Code should apply.

14. Filing of this document may be with an appropriate government entity other than the Secretary of State or County Recorder.

15. If additional provisions are necessary, they should be set forth herein.

16. The signature of the debtor.

17. The signature of the creditor's authorized agent or the creditor.

18. The state where the Security Agreement is signed.

19. The county where the Security Agreement is signed.

20. The date the Security Agreement was notarized.

21. The name of the parties signing the document before the Notary Public.

22. The signature of the Notary Public.

Sample Form
OFFER TO BUY REAL ESTATE

John and Sarah McComb

631 Harper Avenue

1. **TO:**   Chicago, Illinois   (SELLER)[1]

William Windows

818 Westchester Dr.

2. **FROM:**   Chicago, Illinois   (BUYER)[2]

3. **REAL ESTATE:** BUYER hereby offers to purchase real estate in Cook County, Illinois[3] from SELLER as described as follows:

Lot #1 of Bankers First Addition

City of Chicago[4]

4. **SPECIAL ITEMS:** It is understood that the property may be subject to certain easements, zoning requirements, ordinances, restrictive covenants, utility usage, road usage, highway usage, sidewalk usage, etc. This offer is made with the understanding that such special features may be a part of the property. SELLER will provide evidence of any and all special matters through appropriate abstracting upon request.

5. **PURCHASE PRICE:** Purchase price of the aforementioned property shall be $150,000[5], payable by BUYER to SELLER as follows:

6. **TAXES/SPECIAL ASSESSMENTS:** SELLER shall pay all taxes which accrue during the possession of SELLER, and BUYER shall pay all taxes which are accrued subsequent to the possession date set out herein. Any and all special assessments which have accrued during SELLER's possession shall be paid by SELLER. If any special assessments accrue subsequent to the possession date, same shall be paid by BUYER.

7. **INSURANCE**[6]**:** SELLER shall maintain insurance coverage for liability, fire, theft, casualty, tornado and other property damage until the possession date. After the possession date, the BUYER shall be responsible for all insurance upon the premises.

8. **PROPERTY CONDITION:** The SELLER shall preserve the property in its present condition and have property maintained in such condition until the possession date at which time BUYER will assume possession, maintenance and care of the property. Care and maintenance of the property shall include all fixtures of the property, all trees, shrubs, fences, gates, and interior fixtures such as plumbing, heating, electrical, water heaters, water softeners, air conditioning, blinds, awnings, etc.

The form opposite is an example of how a typical form for an Offer to Buy Real Estate may be completed. A blank version of this form (for your use) appears on pages 131–133.

1. The full names of the sellers need to be included. It is also recommended that the address be included.

2. The full name of the buyer should be included, along with the address of the buyer.

3. The county and state location is recommended.

4. A legal discription of the property should be included. The one used is hypothetical.

5. The purchase price should be stated. The price mentioned is hypothetical.

6. Insurance requirements may vary from state to state; therefore, an attorney should be consulted.

Sample Form: Offer to Buy Real Estate *(continued)*

9. **POSSESSION:** If this offer is accepted on or before the 1st[7] day of June[7], 1996[7], at 1:00 o'clock[8] p.m.[9] by the SELLER, BUYER shall have possession of the premises on or before the 1st[10] day of August[10], 1996[10]. During the period prior to BUYER's possession, SELLER shall maintain the property in its present condition and shall not cause the property to decrease in value or allow for any portion of the property to be damaged or destroyed. SELLER shall preserve all aspects of the property including: the integrity of any and all building exteriors, any and all landscaping, fencing, gates, wells, towers and outbuildings. SELLER shall also maintain all interior integrity of all buildings including: heating systems, plumbing, electrical fixtures, doors, screens, awnings, air conditioning equipment, floor coverings, wall coverings, etc.

10. **DEED/BILL OF SALE**[11]**:** Once all terms and conditions, including full payment of the consideration for the above described property, have been fulfilled, the SELLER shall execute and deliver a Warranty Deed to the BUYER. The deed shall convey title in fee simple. The SELLER will also demonstrate merchantable title, provide the BUYER with the abstract to the property showing the original government patent and/or platting, title in the SELLER's name and the disclosure of all easements, restrictions and covenants on the property. The SELLER shall pay the abstracting costs to the date of the BUYER's final payment under this contract. A Bill of Sale shall be executed by the SELLER if any personal property is a part of this conveyance. The deed of conveyance may contain restrictions of qualifications as to zoning, easements, restrictive covenants or specific regulatory matters that restrict use of the property. If the property is held in joint tenancy, the deed provided must properly reflect such ownership and conveyance. A spouse not listed on the title shall be presumed to have relinquished all rights of dower, homestead and distributive share

11. **ENCUMBRANCES**[12]**:** Any and all encumbrances on the property shall be satisfied by SELLER on or before the date of possession as noted above.

12. **FORFEITURE OF DOWN PAYMENT**[13]**:** If the BUYER fails to perform under this contract, any payments made may be forfeited to the SELLER at SELLER's option. If SELLER fails to timely perform, the BUYER shall have all payments returned. Both BUYER and SELLER are entitled to utilize any and all other remedies accorded them under the laws of the State of Illinois[13] for failure to perform the conditions of this contract.

13. **APPLICABLE LAW**[14]**:** The law applicable to the enforcement of this contract is the law of the State of Illinois[14].

The form opposite is an example of how a typical form for an Offer to Buy Real Estate may be completed.

7. The date within which the seller may accept the offer.

8. The time by which the offer must be accepted.

9. Whether the offer needs to be accepted before or after noon.

10. The date of possession.

11. The laws vary between states regarding the requirements for deeds and/or bills of sale; therefore, an attorney should be consulted.

12. Many states require a more complete disclosure relative to the encumbrances that may exist on a property. An attorney should be consulted.

13. Although the language used relative to the forfeiture of down payment is fairly standard, there are certain states which would require a modification of this language.

14. The state under which a contract would be enforced should be stated.

Sample Form: Offer to Buy Real Estate *(continued)*

14. **OTHER PROVISIONS**[15]:

Dated at <u>Chicago, Illinois</u>[16] on this <u>15th</u>[17] day of <u>May</u>[17], <u>1996</u>[17].

_____[18]　　　　_____[19]

BUYER　　　　　　　　　SELLER

_____[18]　　　　_____[19]

BUYER　　　　　　　　　SELLER

STATE OF <u>ILLINOIS</u>[20]　)

　　　　　　　　　　　　　)ss

COUNTY OF <u>COOK</u>[21]　)

On this <u>15th</u>[22] day of <u>May</u>[22] , <u>1996</u>[22], the persons identified above<u>, John McComb,</u> <u>Sarah McComb, and William Windows</u>[23], signed before me, a Notary Public, their signatures when they personally appeared to declare the above voluntary act and deed.

_____[24]

NOTARY PUBLIC

The form opposite is an example of how a typical form for an Offer to Buy Real Estate may be completed.

15. Any additional provisions relative to the offer to buy the real estate should be set forth at this point.

16. The location where the offer was signed should be recited.

17. The date when the offer is made should be indicated.

18. The signature of the buyer should be provided. If there are two buyers, both must sign.

19. The signature of seller(s) must appear on the contract.

20. The state where the parties met before a notary.

21. The county where the notary witnessed the signature of the parties.

22. The date the parties signed before the notary. There may be a separate requirement for acknowledgment by separate notaries as to the sellers and the buyers if the documents are signed in different locations.

23. The parties appearing before the notary should be listed.

24. The signature of the notary.

Sample Form
REAL ESTATE PURCHASE CONTRACT

THIS AGREEMENT, dated this 4th[1] day of May[1] , 1996[1], by and between Robert and Amelia Clinton[2] of 141 Hillview Ave., Reston, Virginia[3], hereafter referred to as the **Buyer**, and John and Gretchen Bell[4] of 924 Marlow Street East, Dale City, Virginia[5], hereafter referred to as the **Seller**, recites the following terms and conditions:

1. **PROMISE TO PURCHASE REAL ESTATE:** The party of the Seller has agreed to sell certain real estate to the party of the Buyer in conjunction with the consideration, terms and conditions of this agreement. This agreement is subject to the various laws of the State of Virginia[6] and may be filed with the appropriate governmental entity in order to provide proper notice to any interested parties and the public.

2. **DESCRIPTION OF PROPERTY:** The property sold by the party of the Seller to the party of the Buyer is legally described as:

Lot #4 and the South100 Ft. of Lot #5

of the Old World Development Tract[7]

The aforementioned property may be subject to various zoning restrictions, easements, restrictive covenants, rules, regulations and laws as a survey of the premises, review of the abstract and the examination of various title documents may demonstrate. The party of the Second Part shall make available to the party of the First Part such documents for review when appropriate or when requested.

3. **CONSIDERATION:** The Buyer shall pay the purchase price of $285,000[8] to the Seller for the above described premises, exclusive of any amounts of interest which may be due by the Buyer to the Seller, pursuant to the following. A down payment of $50,000[9] shall be paid by the Buyer to the Seller on the 4th[10] day of May[10], 1996[10]. The balance of the purchase price, $235,000[11], shall be paid by the Buyer to the Seller plus interest at the rate of 1/2%[12] per month and shall be due on the 5th[13] day of each and every month. The first monthly payment shall be made on the 5th[14] day of June[14], 1996[14] with a payment on the 5th[15] day of every month thereafter until the 5th[16] day of May[16], 2001[16]. At the time of the last payment, any remaining and unpaid balance or balloon payment amount shall be made. The balloon amount, providing all regular payments, taxes, special assessments, etc. have been paid by the Buyer, shall be all remaining sums due including any interest arrearage, any unpaid taxes, and the balance of the unpaid principal[17].

The form opposite is an example of how a typical form for a Real Estate Purchase may be completed. A blank version of this form (for your use) appears on pages 135–138.

1. The date the agreement is signed should be first noted.

2. The full name of the purchaser and the purchaser's spouse should be listed.

3. The address of the purchaser and purchaser's spouse.

4. The full name of the seller and the seller's spouse.

5. The address of the seller and seller's spouse.

6. The state in which the property is located.

7. Legal description of the property being purchased.

8. The total amount of the purchase price should be set forth.

9. The total amount of down payment should be recited.

10. The day the down payment is to be made should be noted.

11. The balance of the purchase price should be set forth.

12. The percent that is allowable by law should be set forth.

13. The day of each month on which the installment payment is due.

14. The day the first monthly payment is due.

15. The day of each month on which each payment is due.

16. The day of the final payment under the contract, exclusive of a balloon payment or balance remaining after the last payment.

17. A balloon payment or the amount due after all of the monthly payments have been made, with appropriate reductions to the principal.

Sample Form: Real Estate Purchase Contract *(continued)*

4. **TAXES/SPECIAL ASSESSMENT:** The Seller shall pay all taxes and any special assessments which have occurred or been assessed on the property up to and including the 5th[18] day of May[18], 1996[18]. The Buyer shall pay all taxes and any special assessments which have accrued or been assessed after the aforementioned date. In conjunction with this provision, the Seller agrees to pay $11,500[19] for any taxes or assessments attributable to his ownership/possession, and the Buyer agrees to pay all other taxes and assessments. If the Buyer fails to pay taxes or assessments when due, the Seller may, to protest interest, pay such amounts. In such event, the Seller may assess the advances plus interest to the Buyer or declare this contract in default in conjunction with the default provision of this contract.

5. **MORTGAGES/ENCUMBRANCES:** The Seller shall, with the proceeds of the payments made by the Buyer, make all payments to other parties who may hold a mortgage or lien in order to satisfy all mortgages and other encumbrances upon the property. The Seller is permitted to make such payments monthly as payments are received from the Buyer. The Buyer shall receive monthly verification from the Seller that the mortgage or other obligations of encumbrances are satisfied to third parties by the Seller. If the Seller fails to provide verification or fails to make the required mortgage or encumbrance payment obligations, the Buyer may make arrangements for the monthly obligation to the Seller under this contract to be paid directly to the party who holds a mortgage or other encumbrance on the property. Once the Buyer has reduced the balance of this contract to the existing mortgage or encumbrance amounts, the Buyer may, if permitted by the party holding the mortgage or encumbrance, either assume the mortgage or encumbrance or pay the monthly amounts directly to the holder of the mortgage or encumbrance. Such payments would occur in the event the Seller's equity interest has been paid to the Seller .

6. **INSURANCE**[20]**:** The Buyer, from the date of possession forward, shall maintain insurance coverage for all liability, fire, tornado, flooding, other hazards and contingencies as the Seller may require on all buildings existing or erected on the above described premises and the contents, if any of the contents have also been sold by the Seller to the Buyer. The Buyer shall obtain an appropriate rider on the insurance policies, with the Seller identified as the owner in fee simple of the premises. In the event of any loss, the Seller must be a co-payee of insurance proceeds in order to assure the proper replacement or repair or loss to the premises.

The form opposite is an example of how a typical form for a Real Estate Purchase may be completed.

18. The taxes for which the seller agrees to be responsible should be included up through the date noted. The date shown is hypothetical.

19. The amount to which the seller has agreed to pay taxes.

20. Each state has various provisions that might change the language set forth in this document; therefore, an attorney should be consulted.

Sample Form: Real Estate Purchase Contract *(continued)*

7. **NEW ENCUMBRANCES/LIENS**[21]**:** Neither party may encumber the above described property in any way during the term of this agreement unless specific written consent is received by the other party.

8. **DEED/BILL OF SALE**[22]**:** Once all terms and conditions, including full payment of the consideration for the above described property, have been fulfilled, the Seller shall execute and deliver a Warranty Deed to the Buyer. The deed shall convey title in fee simple. The Seller will also demonstrate merchantable title, provide the Buyer with the abstract to the property showing the original government patent and/or platting, title in the Seller's name and the disclosure of all easements, restrictions and covenants on the property. The Seller shall pay the abstracting costs to the date of the Buyer's final payment under this contract. A Bill of Sale shall be executed by the Seller if any personal property is a part of this conveyance. The deed of conveyance may contain restrictions or qualifications as to zoning, easements, restrictive covenants or specific regulatory matters that restrict use of the property. If the property is held in joint tenancy, the deed provided must properly reflect such ownership and conveyance.

9. **FORFEITURE/FORECLOSURE**[23]**:** If the Buyer fails to perform any portion of this contract, as agreed, the Seller may take appropriate action to reclaim the property including the legal action of contract forfeiture. In the event forfeiture is necessary, the Seller shall also be entitled to attorney fees and costs. The failure of any of the following may constitute grounds for forfeiture: (a) payment of amounts due under this contract; (b) payment of taxes and/or special assessments; (c) maintaining insurance; (d) maintaining the premises in good condition and/or reasonable repair; (e) using the premises for lawful purposes; (f) complying with applicable Virginia law regarding use of the premises and; (g) complying with the provision of this contract. Additionally, the failure to comply with the provision of this agreement by the Buyer, shall give the Seller the right to issue a 30[24] day notice to accelerate the payment of the entire balance of this contract.

10. **INTEREST ON DELINQUENCY:** On any amounts deemed to be delinquent by either party under this contract, 6[25]% interest per annum may be applied on such delinquent amounts.

11. **POSSESSION:** The Buyer shall take possession of the premises on the 5th[26] day of May[26], 1996[26].

12. **APPLICABLE LAW:** The laws of the State of Virginia[27] shall govern the terms and conditions of this contract.

The form opposite is an example of how a typical form for a Real Estate Purchase may be completed.

21. Often it is wise to fully disclose any encumbrances or liens, and if so, a recitation of the state law may be included.

22. Compliance with state law is important relative to any conveyance involving a deed or bill of sale.

23. Forfeiture or foreclosure may well vary between states; therefore, an attorney should be consulted.

24. A 30 day notice has been arbitrarily selected for the purpose of this sample contract.

25. The interest rate is set forth.

26. The date of possession is set forth.

27. The state of applicable law is set forth.

Sample Form: Real Estate Purchase Contract *(continued)*

13. **OTHER PROVISIONS**[28]:

Dated at <u>Dale City, Virginia</u>[29] this <u>4th</u>[30] day of <u>May</u>[30], <u>1996</u>[30].

_____   _____

_____   _____

_____[31]   _____[33]

Name and Address of Seller   Name and Address of Buyer

_____   _____

_____   _____

_____[32]   _____[34]

Name and Address of Spouse   Name and Address of Spouse

STATE OF <u>Virginia</u>[35]   )

)

COUNTY OF <u>Prince William</u>[36]   )

On this <u>4th</u>[37] day of <u>May</u>[37], <u>1996</u>[37], the persons identified above, <u>John Bell, Gretchen Bell, Robert Clinton, and Amelia Clinton</u>[38], signed before me, a Notary Public, their signatures when they personally appeared to declare the above voluntary act and deed.

_____[39]

NOTARY PUBLIC

The form opposite is an example of how a typical form for a Real Estate Purchase may be completed.

28. If any additional provisions are required, they should be set forth.

29. The location where the contract is signed should be set forth.

30. The date the contract is signed should be recited.

31. The name and address of the seller.

32. The name and address of the spouse of the seller.

33. The name and address of the buyer.

34. The name and address of the spouse of the buyer.

35. The state where the contract is signed before a notary. This may require two verifications if the sellers sign in one state and the buyers sign in another.

36. The county where the parties have signed the contract.

37. The date the contract was signed.

38. The parties who signed the contract before the notary.

39. The signature of the notary.

Sample Form
BILL OF SALE

THIS AGREEMENT between Eileen Smith[1] of 21 Mead St., South Bend, Indiana[2], hereinafter SELLER, and Grace Auburn[3] of 22 Big Ten St., Mishawaka, Indiana[4], hereinafter BUYER, is for the sale of the following:

a storage facility located upon the premises at Lots #4, 5, 6, and 7 of the Regents' Third Addition to The City of South Bend, all yard equipment as shown on Attachment A and all equipment as shown on Attachment B at said premises[5].

1. **PROPERTY AS IS**[6]**:** The property as described above is sold by the SELLER to the BUYER as the property is seen and observed with any and all faults which it may have.

2. **PURCHASE PRICE:** The BUYER agrees to pay to the SELLER, at SELLER's address, the amount of $130,000[7]. Payment shall be made by the BUYER to the SELLER in the following manner:

      a.) $30,000 at the time this agreement is signed[8],
      b.) $25,000 on May 15, 1997
      c.) $25,000 on May 15, 1998
      d.) $25,000 on May 15, 1999
      e.) $25,000 on May 15, 2000

3. **DEFAULT**[9]**:** In the event BUYER fails to make payment or is otherwise in default in paying the SELLER, the SELLER has all rights to reclaim the property and/or the SELLER may declare the entire balance due, if any sums are left unpaid.

4. **INTEREST RATE:** The interest rate for any unpaid sums shall be the rate of 8[10]% per annum.

The form opposite is an example of how a typical form for a Bill of Sale may be completed. A blank version of this form (for your use) appears on pages 139–140.

1. The full name of the seller should be set forth.

2. The location or address of the seller.

3. The full name of the buyer.

4. The location or address of the buyer.

5. A description of the property sold.

6. Number 1 is sometimes used as a disclaimer and, in some states, may require a more specific description as to the condition of the property.

7. The total purchase price of the property should be set forth.

8. A hypothetical method of payment is set forth.

9. In the event of default, certain provisions of the state's Uniform Commercial Code or Consumer Credit Code may have an effect; therefore, an attorney should be consulted.

10. An arbitrary rate of interest has been set forth in this particular sample; however, an interest rate in full compliance with state statutes should normally be set forth.

Sample Form: Bill of Sale *(continued)*

5. **DELIVERY OF PROPERTY**[11]**:** In the event of default, at the demand of SELLER, the BUYER must deliver the goods to the SELLER at the address listed above and in the same condition in which BUYER acquired the property from SELLER.

Dated this 15th[12] day of May[12], 1996[12], at South Bend, Indiana[13].

_____[14]   _____[15]
BUYER   SELLER

STATE OF INDIANA[16]   )
)ss
COUNTY OF ST. JOSEPH[17])

On this 15th[18] day of May[18], 1996[18], the persons identified above, Eileen Smith, Grace Auburn[19], signed before me, a Notary Public, their signatures when they personally appeared to declare the above voluntary act and deed.

_____[20]
NOTARY PUBLIC

The form opposite is an example of how a typical form for a Bill of Sale may be completed.

11. Delivery of the property may vary from state to state. Accordingly, an attorney should be consulted.

12. The date the transaction is signed.

13. The location of the transaction.

14. The signature of the buyer.

15. The signature of the seller.

16. The state in which the parties signed the document.

17. The county in which the document was signed.

18. The date on which the document was signed.

19. The names of the parties signing the document before the notary.

20. The signature of the notary.

Sample Form
SUBCONTRACTOR PERFORMANCE AGREEMENT FOR RESIDENTIAL CONSTRUCTION (<u>ELECTRICAL WORK</u>)[1]

THIS AGREEMENT, entered this <u>15th</u>[2] day of <u>June</u>[2], <u>1996</u>[2], between <u>Glen Wilder</u>[3] of <u>103 Plainview St., Albion, Idaho</u>[4] and <u>Eldon Johnson</u>[5] of <u>American Falls, Idaho</u>[6], is established and conditioned on the following terms:

1. **<u>PARTY STATUS</u>:** Owner shall serve as the general contractor on the building project described in paragraph two herein. Subcontractor shall serve in his own capacity as a legal entity known as an Independent Contractor and, accordingly, shall employ, compensate and manage any assistance required for performance of this contract. Subcontractor shall be responsible for: liability insurance for work related to this project, workers' compensation for its employees, appropriate tax withholding (federal, state and local), appropriate job service taxes(federal, state and local), and all union relations. Subcontractor shall hold owner/builder harmless and thereby indemnify owner/builder for any claims made which may be generated from work related to this project.

2. **<u>JOB SITE</u>:** The job site for this project shall be kept free of debris, trash, dangerous conditions, and potential hazards by subcontractor, and said subcontractor shall leave the following described premises in a clean and injury-free environment at the conclusion of each work day. The job site premises is described as follows:

<u>80 Millriver Road</u>
<u>American Falls, Idaho</u>[7]

3. **<u>COMPLIANCE STANDARDS</u>**[8]**:** Subcontractor shall comply with all federal, state and local laws, rules and regulations including, but not limited to, OSHA standards. Subcontractor shall hold owner/builder harmless for any violations and shall, accordingly, indemnify said owner/builder.

4. **<u>TERM</u>:** The term of this agreement is for the construction period required for the construction of the aforementioned project (described in paragraph 2). Limitation and deadlines on said project are as follows:

a) 50% of the "rough in" work to be performed by subcontractor shall be completed by the <u>1st</u>[9] day of <u>September</u>[9], <u>1996</u>[9].

b) An additional 30% of the total amount of the work to be performed by subcontractor shall be completed by the <u>15th</u>[10] day of <u>October</u>[10], <u>1996</u>[10].

The form opposite is an example of how a typical form for a Subcontractor Performance Agreement may be completed. A blank version of this form (for your use) appears on pages 141–144.

1. The type of subcontracting work to be performed should be set forth.

2. The date on which the contract is entered.

3. The name of the owner or builder. In this case, it is the owner.

4. The address of the owner or builder.

5. The name of the subcontractor or the subcontractor's company or both. In this case, it is an individual subcontractor.

6. The address of the subcontractor.

7. The location at which the work will be completed.

8. There may be various compliance standards which are unique to each state or locality; therefore, an attorney should be consulted regarding these matters.

9. An arbitrary date was selected for the completion of 50% of the work.

10. October 15, 1996, was arbitrarily selected for the subcontractor to have completed an additional 30% of the work.

Sample Form: Subcontractor Performance Agreement (continued)

c) The final 20% of the total work to be performed by subcontractor shall be completed by the 15th[11] day of November[11], 1996[11].

d) In the event the work to be performed as set forth above is not completed as stated, the liquidated damages provision of this agreement shall apply[12].

5. **LIQUIDATED DAMAGES:** In the event subcontractor fails to perform in conjunction with the workmanship provision (paragraph 7) or any other provision of this agreement or if there is a failure to meet the deadlines set out in paragraph 4 (or as modified in paragraph 6 herein), subcontractor shall be penalized the sum of $500[13] per day.

6. **WEATHER DAYS:** Only in the event the parties agree in writing to extensions for bad weather days will exceptions be allowed for the deadlines of paragraph 4 or the liquidated damages of paragraph 5 above. Weather day extensions will not be unreasonably withheld by owner/contractor; however, such extensions must be for good cause shown since the parties in this agreement contemplate that 15 bad weather days have already been included in the deadlines set forth in paragraph 4 above.

7. **WORKMANSHIP**[14]**:** Subcontractor agrees to provide lasting and quality work for the items set forth in the attached "estimate " or "quote" for services. Said work will be subject to the approval of owner/builder prior to payment for said services. Subcontractor warrants his work and will make or pay for any and all repairs or corrections which are necessary due to faulty or improper craftsmanship.

8. **MATERIALS:** Subcontractor shall provide all quality material necessary for the work on the project (premises) described in paragraph two above subject to the following:

Builder Wilder shall provide all conduit for project
from owner's personal business[15].

Owner/builder will pay to subcontractor the total sum of $5,845[16] as set forth in the attached "estimate" or "quote" and no more, unless a change order is made and signed by the parties for any items not included in the attached "estimate" or "quote." Without a change order duly executed, any additional items will be provided by subcontractor at subcontractor's expense. Payment shall be made by owner/contractor to subcontractor on the following basis:

	AMOUNT	DATE	PERCENTAGE OF COMPLETION
a)	$1,000	9/1/96	50%[17]
b)	$2,000	10/15/96	30%[18]
c)	$2,845	11/15/96	20%[19]

10. **EMPLOYEES:** Subcontractor may, at his discretion, hire additional help to assist on the aforementioned project; however, any such assistance will be paid by

The form opposite is an example of how a typical form for a Subcontractor Performance Agreement may be completed.

11. November 15, 1996 was the date selected for the final 20% of the work.

12. This provision is set forth to let the parties know that liquidated damages will be charged for any delay where the subcontractor fails to complete the project within the specified period of time and for which an extention has not been granted.

13. The amount set forth is an arbitrary figure which is used to delineate the amount of liquidated damages. In this case, it is on a daily basis.

14. The workmanship may vary from location to location. It is certainly possible for this provision to be more elaborate.

15. An exception to a normal contract project was set forth as a hypothetical example, wherein, the owner was to provide conduit.

16. The total amount of payment was set forth.

17. The first installment of payment, the date of installment, and the percentage of completion has been set forth.

18. An amount to be paid on the second installment payment of 10/15/96 was set forth after 30% of the electrical project had been completed.

19. The final payment on 11/15/96 was set forth when the final 20% was completed. This, of course, is a hypothetical example.

Sample Form: Subcontractor Performance Agreement *(continued)*

subcontractor. Payment for additional help shall be the sole obligation of subcontractor, and such payment shall include, but is not limited to: all taxes, withholding, job service, workers' compensation and any other governmental obligations, as well as, salaries which subcontractor is required to pay.

11. **INSURANCE**[20]: Subcontractor shall maintain all appropriate forms of insurance including, but not limited to: workers' compensation, health and accident, general liability and any other form of insurance requested by owner/builder. Owner/builder shall be listed as a protected party under such policies of insurance. Subcontractor shall hold owner/builder harmless for any accident which may occur "on" or "to and from" the job site which, in any way, relates to subcontractor's work on the aforementioned project. Proof of insurance coverage shall be provided to owner/builder within 20 days after the signing of this agreement. Commencement of this project will not occur until subcontractor has provided proof of insured coverage.

12. **RIGHT TO INSPECT:** Owner/builder shall have the right to inspect the project at all times and the additional right to stop the project and terminate this agreement if subcontractor's work is not done in a workmanlike and quality manner acceptable to owner/builder.

13. **LIEN WAIVERS**[21]: The contractor shall provide to the owner appropriate lien waivers upon receipt of payment as set forth in paragraph 9 above.

14. **ADDITIONAL PROVISIONS**[22]:

a)   none[22]

b)

c)

Dated this 1st[23] day of July[23], 1996[23].

_____[24]   _____[25]

SUBCONTRACTOR   OWNER/BUILDER

_____[26]   _____[27]

WITNESS   WITNESS

This is not a substitute for legal advice. An attorney must be consulted.

Copyright © 1996 by LAW™

The form opposite is an example of how a typical form for a Subcontractor Performance Agreement may be completed.

20. Insurance requirements may vary from state to state or from location to location; therefore, an attorney should be consulted regarding this matter.

21. Lien waivers and the requirements for lien waivers may vary from state to state. Accordingly, an attorney should be consulted.

22. No additional provisions were set forth as a sample in this case. However, space has been provided for any additional provisions to this agreement.

23. The date the agreement was signed should be set forth.

24. The signature of the subcontractor, in this case, the electrician.

25. The signature of the owner or builder should be provided.

26. Space for a witness who observed the contractor's signature of this contract.

27. Space for a witness who observed the owner's signature of this contract.

Sample Form
DEADLINE EXTENSION AMENDMENT

The parties in authority as identified below hereby agree to amend the subcontractor performance agreement for residential construction:

a) 15 Bad Weather Days which are identified in paragraph 6 of the subcontractor performance agreement which have already occurred are:

	Day of Week	Date	Owner/Contractor Initials	Subcontractor Initials
1.	Monday[1]	8/12/96[1]	_____[1]	_____[1]
2.				
3.				
4.				
5.				
6.				
7.				
8.				
9.				
10.				
11.				
12.				
13.				
14.				
15.				

b) The total of 1[2] additional days will be permitted as an extension to the deadlines set forth in paragraph 4 of the subcontractor performance agreement before liquidated damages(paragraph 5 of said contract) are imposed.

Dated at Rockland, Idaho[3] on this 13th[4] day of August[4], 1996[4].

_____[5]   _____[6]

Owner/Contractor   Subcontractor

The form opposite is an example of how a typical form for a Deadline Extension Amendment may be completed. A blank version of this form (for your use) appears on page 145.

1. The purpose of a Deadline Extension Amendment is to allow the flexibility for additional bad weather days, etc., which may be encountered by a contractor. In this particular case, there was only one exception allowed for one such day, which would give the contractor an additional day beyond his deadline of the original agreement. If the reader will look back to the Subcontractor Performance Agreement, the reader will note that there is a provision in Paragraph 6 for weather days and in Paragraph 5 for liquidated damages. Generally, a Deadline Extension Amendment would allow the contractor additional days beyond the deadline, thereby eliminating liquidated damages on the days for which exceptions are allowed.

2. Only 1 additional day was hypothetically noted in this case.

3. The location where the Deadline Extension Amendment is signed should be noted. In this case, a hypothetical city was used.

4. The date the agreement is signed should be noted.

5. The signature of the owner/contractor.

6. The signature of the subcontractor.

Sample Form
WAIVER OF LIEN[1]

The undersigned contractor of <u>American Falls</u>[2], <u>Idaho</u>[2], does hereby provide the following waiver of any and all liens on the construction project at <u>1111 5th Avenue</u>[3] in <u>Arbon</u>[4], <u>Idaho</u>[5], to <u>Glen Wilder</u>[6], the (<u>owner/contractor</u>):

1. The parties have previously entered into a construction project for labor and/or materials as shown on the attached estimate and/or attached description;

2. The attached documents contain a description of any and all work that was to be performed at the aforementioned project;

3. The work has been performed and the materials provided in conjunction with the complete agreement(s);

4. In consideration of <u>One thousand eight hundred forty-five</u>[7] Dollars(<u>$1,845</u>[8]) receipt of which is hereby acknowledged as payment in <u>part</u>[9](<u>full/part</u>), the undersigned contractor waives all claims of lien and right of lien that he may obtain against such property by having performed the services described on the attached.

IN WITNESS WHEREOF, the undersigned contractor executes this waiver and release on this <u>1st</u>[10] day of <u>September</u>[10], <u>1996</u>[10].

_____[11]

WITNESS

_____[12]

CONTRACTOR

The form opposite is an example of how a typical form for the Waiver of a Lien may be completed. A blank version of this form (for your use) appears on page 147.

1. Lien waivers may vary from state to state and are regulated specifically by each individual state. In this case, a general format has been used for the Waiver of Lien.

2. The contractor's address is set forth.

3. The address of the location by street is indicated.

4. The city location.

5. The state location.

6. The waiver is given to the owner. In this case, the owner is Glen Wilder.

7. The consideration is the amount of the first installment.

8. The amount of consideration should be noted numerically, as well as being written out.

9. A part installment was noted in this hypothetical situation.

10. The date on which the Lien Waiver is signed is noted.

11. The signature of a witness.

12. The signature of the contractor.

Blank Forms

The forms in this chapter are blank versions of the completed forms in Chapter 4; these forms are for your use.

Form One

APARTMENT LEASE

THIS AGREEMENT, dated this _____ day of _____, 19___, by and between _____ of _____, hereinafter referred to as tenant, and _____of _____, hereinafter referred to as landlord, recite the following terms and conditions:

1. **THE DESCRIPTION OF PREMISES:** Tenant hereby agrees to rent the premises described as follows:

2. **TERM:** Tenant agrees to lease the above described premises for a period of _____ (months) (years) commencing on the _____ day of _____, 19___, and ending on the _____ day of _____, 19___.

3. **RENTAL AMOUNT:** Tenant agrees to rent the aforementioned premises for the amount of $_____ per month payable on the _____ day of each month after the _____ day of _____, 19___, the date of the first rental payment.

4. **SPECIAL CONDITIONS:** Tenant agrees to be bound by the special conditions for the premises as set out in the attached Rules and Regulations.

5. **CONDITION OF PREMISES:** Tenant agrees to maintain the premises in good condition at all times during possession and shall be certain that the premises are maintained in the condition as the premises were when first received by the tenant. In the event there are any problems with the premises which involve damage of any sort, the tenant must bring such matters to the immediate attention of the landlord.

6. **DAMAGE DEPOSIT:** Tenant agrees to place with the landlord a damage deposit equal to one month's rent, which amount is $_____.

7. **SURRENDER OF PREMISES:** Tenant shall surrender the premises to Landlord immediately upon termination of this agreement.

8. **TERMINATION:** In the event tenant fails to perform any of the conditions of this Lease, the landlord shall have the option to provide notice to the tenant of tenant's failure to comply. Landlord shall have the rights of the three day notice to quit in the event of non-compliance with this agreement or in the event of nonpayment of rent in conjunction with this lease.

9. **USE:** Tenant shall use the premises for _____ (purpose) only and may not use the premise for any other purpose without the expressed written consent of Landlord.

10. **RIGHT TO ENTER:** Landlord shall have the right to enter the premises at any reasonable time for the purpose of inspection.

11. **APPLICABLE LAW:** The law that governs this Agreement is the law of the State of _____. In the event the landlord finds it necessary to enforce the provisions of this agreement against the tenant, the landlord shall be entitled to reasonable attorney's fees and costs.

12. **ADDITIONAL PROVISIONS:**

_____   _____
TENANT   LANDLORD

This is not a substitute for legal advice. An attorney must be consulted.

Form Two

TYPICAL APARTMENT RULES AND REGULATIONS

1.) Tenant shall keep premises in good condition.

2.) Tenant shall not interfere with other tenant's premises.

3.) Tenant shall pay rent promptly on the due date.

4.) Tenant shall not make any alterations to the premises without written permission of the landlord.

5.) Tenant shall keep proper liability, fire and/or other damage insurance on the contents of the premises leased.

6.) Tenant shall not receive a refund of the damage deposit until landlord is certain that the premises are free of damages upon the surrender of the premises.

7.) No tenant shall interfere in any manner with any portion either of the heating or lighting or other apparatus in or about the building.

8.) Automobiles must be kept within yellow lines of the parking lot areas.

9.) Sanitary napkins shall not be deposited in toilets but shall be wrapped and deposited with other waste matter and refuse.

10.) Tenant shall be responsible for closing of windows in his or her apartment during storms.

11.) Doors to apartments shall be kept closed at all times.

12.) Owner shall have the right to inspect apartment at reasonable times.

13.) There shall be no door-to-door soliciting of any kind on said premises.

14.) Owner shall furnish extra keys and replace lost keys for $1.00 each. Upon the expiration of lease, tenant shall account for all keys delivered by owner.

15.) The landlord reserves the right: (1) to change any of the foregoing rules by rescinding or amending, or (2) to make such other rules or regulations as are deemed necessary to provide for the comfort and convenience of all tenants, and for the safety, care, proper maintenance and cleanliness of the premises.

16.) It is recommended that garbage disposal covers be kept in the drain position when the unit is not in use. This will prevent foreign material from dropping accidentally into the waste disposal unit. In using the equipment, be sure the cold water is turned on. It is important to maintain a sufficient flow of water to flush shredded waste, even after the disposal has been turned off. Please do not attempt to insert corn cobs, bottle caps, glass, pins, foil, crockery, rugs, string or paper into the disposal as this may cause malfunction and consequent inconvenience to you. Clogged disposal will be unclogged and/or repaired at the expense of the tenant.

17.) Laundry rooms are equipped with coin-operated washers and dryers. Kindly remove clothes promptly from machine. Do not use tints or dyes in the units. Please follow operating instructions and report any difficulty whatsoever.

18.) No doormats or other obstructions should be placed at your entrance door. Mail or paper deliveries should be taken in as soon as possible to minimizes the possibility of accidents to passersby.

19.) Please advise owner promptly of any malfunctions or difficulties so that repairs and/or adjustments can be made at the least inconvenience to you.

20.) Nothing shall be attached to walls or woodwork except the stick-on type fasteners or small nails driven at an angle.

Form Three

BUSINESS LEASE AGREEMENT

This **LEASE AGREEMENT**, executed in duplicate, made and entered into this _____ day of _____, 19___, by and between _____, (first party) of _____, (first party's address) hereinafter called "LESSOR," and _____, (second party) of _____, (second party's address), hereinafter called "LESSEE."

WITNESSETH

1. **PREMISES:** LESSOR, in consideration of the rents herein agreed to be paid and in conjunction with the agreements and conditions herein contained, does hereby demise and lease unto LESSEE the following described premises:

(here describe premises to be leased)

2. **RENT:** LESSEE shall pay to LESSOR on the first day of each month from the _____ day of _____, 19___, up to and including the _____ day of _____, 20___, for the premises in paragraph one of this Lease, in the amount of $_____ each month. Rent may be adjusted every year by the LESSOR and will be tied to the mortgage rate of a major lending institution.

3. **TERM:** The term of this lease shall be for a period of _____ years commencing on the _____ day of _____, 19___, and shall end on the _____ day of _____, 20___, or on such earlier date pursuant to this written agreement or this lease may be terminated pursuant to the conditions of this Lease or pursuant to law.

4. **USE:** The leased premises shall be used for _____ for the conduct of the business of the LESSEE. LESSEE, agrees that leased premises shall not be used for any immoral or unlawful purposes, nor shall the premises be used for sleeping or living purposes, or in any manner that may tend to increase the risk of fire, other dangers or insurance rates.

5. **UTILITIES:** The LESSEE agrees to provide payment for all utilities. LESSOR shall not be liable for stoppage of any utility services including stoppages for needed repair or improvements or any cause beyond LESSOR's control.

6. **LIABILITY FOR INJURY:** LESSOR shall not be liable or responsible for any accident or injury to the person or property of LESSEE or anyone else that may arise from, or on, said premises. This provision shall apply to damage caused by water, snow, frost, steam, sewage, sewer gas or odors, bursting or leaking pipes, faucets and plumbing fixtures, and shall apply without distinction as to whose act nor neglect is responsible for the damage and whether the same was due to the specifically enumerated above or to some other cause of an entirely different kind. LESSEE is to hold LESSOR harmless for any damages to any person or persons caused by or resulting in any way from LESSEE's negligence or that of any person in LESSEE's employ or any persons on said premises by the permission or invitation of LESSEE. LESSEE should have no claim for damages resulting from any defect in the leased premises, unless the LESSOR shall have failed to remedy such defect within reasonable time after receiving written notice from the LESSEE of its existence.

7. **FIRE INSURANCE AND WAIVER OF SUBROGATION:** LESSOR shall cause each insurance policy carried by LESSOR to include protection for the demised premises against loss by fire and other causes covered by standard extended coverage, and LESSEE shall do the same. Such insurance shall be written in a manner so as to provide that the insurance carrier waives all right of recovery by way of subrogation against LESSOR or LESSEE in connection with any loss or damage covered by any such policies. Neither party shall be liable to the other for any loss or damage caused by fire or any of the risks enumerated in standard extended coverage insurance. However, if such waiver cannot be obtained or is obtainable only by the payment of an additional premium, the party undertaking such insurance coverage shall have a period of ten(10) days after the giving of such notice either to: (a) place such insurance in companies which are reasonably satisfactory to the other party and will carry such insurance with wavier of subrogation, or (b) agree to pay such additional premium if such policy is obtainable at additional cost. If the release of either the LESSOR or LESSEE as set forth in the second sentence of this paragraph shall contravene any law with respect to exculpatory agreements, the liability of the LESSOR or LESSEE, as the case may be, shall be deemed not released but shall be deemed secondary to that of the insurer.

8. **ALTERATIONS:** The premises shall not be altered or changed without written consent of the LESSOR, and all alterations or improvements or additions desired by the LESSEE and to which LESSOR has agreed shall be made under the direction of the LESSOR but at the expense of the LESSEE. All improvements, alterations or additions (except_____) shall, in the absence of written agreement to the

contrary, remain on and be surrendered with the premises at the expiration of the term of this lease by lapse of time or otherwise.

9. **MAINTENANCE AND REPAIRS:** LESSEE shall make all repairs to the demised premises including, but not limited to: plumbing, heating, electrical and air conditioning equipment repairs.

10. **ABATEMENT:** LESSEE shall not be entitled to compensation or abatement of rent because of any inconvenience or annoyance arising from the making of repairs or the alteration to the building, or from any work done at the building, or other operations conducted on structures erected on any adjacent building or the premises, or because of interference with view, light, air or wire by reason thereof.

11. **RENT IN CASE OF CASUALTY:** If the premises be rendered untenable by fire, wind, storm, or other cause, no rent shall accrue until the premises are again ready for occupancy providing any such damage shall not be the fault or negligence of the LESSEE or LESSEE's employees or licensees. In case the premises are not restored to tenantable condition within one hundred twenty(120) days after such casualty, either party may terminate this lease and the rent shall be apportioned and paid to the time that the premises became untenable.

12. **ASSIGNMENT:** This lease may not be assigned, nor any part of the leased premises sublet to anyone without the LESSOR's expressed written consent. No extension or alteration of this lease shall be binding unless the same is in writing and signed by both parties hereto.

13. **WAIVER:** Waiver of any portion of any of the provisions of this lease shall not constitute a waiver of any other portion.

14. **HOLDING OVER:** If the LESSOR, without executing a new written lease shall allow the LESSEE to remain in possession of the premises after the expiration of this lease, the LESSEE shall become a tenant from month-to-month, under the same conditions of this lease except as to the duration. Any such tenancy may be terminated through the transmittal of thirty(30)days' written notice by either party.

15. **SURRENDER:** Upon the expiration or any earlier termination of this lease, LESSEE shall surrender the leased premises to LESSOR in the good order and condition as received upon the date of the commencement of this lease, reasonable wear and tear excepted.

16. **INTEREST ON UNPAID SUMS:** LESSEE agrees that any and all sums due hereunder and unpaid when due shall draw interest after the due date at the rate of ten percent(10%) per annum, and that all sums unpaid by the _____ day of each month shall be adjusted to include a ten percent(10%) penalty.

17. **LIEN DUE TO UNPAID SUMS:** LESSEE hereby agrees that the rent and/or rental penalties, whether due or to become due shall be a lien on any or all furniture and other property had or used on said premises at any time during the LESSEE's occupancy of the premises. It is mutually agreed that if any of the rent herein specified shall not be paid when due, or if there is a breach of any covenants contained in this agreement, it shall be optional with the LESSOR, at any time, to declare this lease void, and upon giving LESSEE three(3) days' Notice to Quit, as provided by law, to reenter said premises and remove all persons under an appropriate remedy under law including forcible entry or detinue. It is agreed that, in the event suit is commenced to collect rent or any part thereof, or to enforce any provision of this lease, or if suit is brought either by or against the LESSOR for any cause resulting from this lease, reasonable attorney fees shall be paid in addition to all other costs.

18. **PROPERTY AND MERCHANDISE:** LESSEE agrees that all property, goods or merchandise brought, deposited, stored or permitted by LESSEE to be present upon the premises shall be present at the exclusive liability and risk of the LESSEE.

19. **FIXTURES:** LESSEE agrees to repair or replace as applicable, all doors, windows, plumbing, gas, electric, steam or other fixtures broken or otherwise damaged on said premises during the use and tenancy by LESSEE.

20. **QUIET AND ENJOYMENT:** LESSOR represents and warrants to LESSEE that LESSOR has title in fee simple to the leased premises and that so long as LESSEE is paying rent and observing the covenants of this lease, the LESSEE shall quietly hold and enjoy the leased premises in the terms hereof.

21. **COMPLIANCE WITH LAWS:** LESSOR further represents and warrants that the building in which the leased premises are located, and the parking area, comply with applicable zoning and building regulations and that the LESSEE's use thereof in accordance with the provisions of this lease is permitted by such regulations.

22. **ADDITIONAL RULES:** The LESSOR reserves the right, when conditions warrant, to make additional rules governing LESSEE and its employees relating to the proper care of the building and preservation of good order.

23. **MODIFICATION OF LEASE:** The terms, covenants and conditions hereof may not be changed orally but only by an agreement in writing signed by the parties.

24. **SUCCESSOR AND ASSIGNS:** The terms, covenants and conditions of this lease shall be binding upon and shall inure to the benefit of LESSOR and LESSEE and their respective executors, administrators, heirs, distributees, legal representatives, successor and assigns.

25. **PARAGRAPH HEADING:** The paragraph headings herein contained are inserted only as a matter of convenience and for reference and, in no way, define, limit or describe the scope or intent of the lease or, in any way, affect the terms and provisions hereof.

26. **INSPECTION:** It is herein acknowledged that LESSEE has inspected the premises and accepts them in good order.

27. **OPTION TO RENEW:** Upon satisfaction of this initial duration lease ending on the _____ day of _____, 20___, LESSEE is granted an option to renew for an additional _____ year period under the same terms and conditions. The exercise of this option requires that LESSEE furnish LESSOR with written notice of intent to renew no less than sixty(60) days prior to renewal date.

28. **ADDITIONAL PROVISIONS:**

IN WITNESS WHEREOF, the parties hereto duly executed this lease in duplicate the day and year first above written.

_____   _____

Owner of Premises   Second Party-Lessee
First Party-Lessor

_____   _____

Co-owner of Premises   Second Party-Co-Lessee
First Party-Lessor

Form Four

FARM LEASE AGREEMENT

THIS AGREEMENT, dated this _____ day of _____, 19___, by and between (<u>name of the landlord</u>) of (<u>address of landlord</u>), hereinafter referred to as the FIRST PARTY and (<u>name of the lessee</u>) of (<u>address of lessee</u>), hereinafter referred to as SECOND PARTY, recite the following terms and conditions:

1. **<u>LEASED PREMISES:</u>** The FIRST PARTY in conjunction with the conditions contained herein does lease to the SECOND PARTY the following described real estate which is located in _____ County, _____:

(Legal description)

2. **<u>LEASE PERIOD:</u>** This lease shall commence on the _____ day of _____, 19___, and shall continue for _____ year(s) ending on the _____ day of _____, 19___. If this agreement is not terminated by either party in conjunction with the terms and conditions contained herein, it will automatically be renewed under the same terms and conditions for a period of one year, and if the lease is not renewed at the end of that year, it shall continue on a year-to-year basis under the same terms and conditions, providing same is not terminated or modified by the parties in writing.

3. **<u>RENTAL TERMS:</u>** The SECOND PARTY agrees to pay the FIRST PARTY as rent for the above described real estate at the address of the FIRST PARTY, according to the following:

4. **<u>CROP PRESENTATION:</u>** The SECOND PARTY shall prepare annually a crop plan and shall present same to the FIRST PARTY on or before the first day of February of each year during the terms of this agreement. The crop plan shall provide a rationale for crop rotation, soil preservation and conservation, the means by which tilling will occur; a soil erosion control plan which includes maintenance of water courses, waterways, ditches, drainage areas, tiles, etc; and a method of crop production which allows for proper crop rotation during various crop seasons. The SECOND PARTY shall also annually provide a presentation as to the manner in which all crops will be harvested, cultivated and fertilized.

Any use of commercial fertilizer, pesticides, insecticides and use of mineral additives to the soil will need to be included in the crop program annually by the SECOND PARTY for the review and approval of the FIRST PARTY. Any use of potash, phosphate, urea, dap, lime and other trace materials shall be included in an allocation plan during the term of the lease and a proposal by the SECOND PARTY to the FIRST PARTY and shall include a proposal relative to the payment of any minerals, etc. In the event the SECOND PARTY fails to perform in conjunction with the terms of this agreement or in conjunction with the crop presentation plan, as noted above, the FIRST PARTY reserves the right to enter the premises and allow for the proper care and harvest of all crops with appropriate costs for such care and harvest to the SECOND PARTY.

5. **PREMISES CONDITION:** Tenant shall always maintain the best practices relative to the condition of the premises including all land and buildings, fences, roads, tile, wells,_____. The SECOND PARTY shall assure that the above leased premises is maintained in good order and good condition. The premises must always be in substantially the same condition as received by the SECOND PARTY from the FIRST PARTY at the time this lease commenced.

6. **MACHINERY USE AND EQUIPMENT USE:** The cost of all machinery and equipment usage on the premises shall be at the expense of the SECOND PARTY, and such expense shall include the costs of all combining, shelling, harvesting, bailing and/or otherwise acquisition of crops from the premises. The maintenance and cost of the machinery, including all and any repairs, shall be paid by the SECOND PARTY. The SECOND PARTY, however, shall be permitted to use all buildings on the premises for storage of equipment and machinery with the exception of the following:

7. **SITE CARE:** The care of all buildings, roadways, trees, shrubs, grass, utility lines and other features placed upon the above described real estate shall be preserved and provided appropriate care by the SECOND PARTY; however, the application of paint, carpentry items and other repairs shall be paid by the FIRST PARTY on receipt of notice from the SECOND PARTY. Any such needs for repairs such as carpentry and/or paint, etc. should be paid by the FIRST PARTY after appropriate notice from the SECOND PARTY and after approval by the FIRST PARTY.

8. **TERMINATION:** As provided in the provision relative to term noted above, the period of this agreement is for _____ year(s). It may be renewed, if not terminated by either of the parties, for _____ year periods if a new written lease agreement is not signed between the parties. This agreement shall automatically become null and void if the parties prepare an agreement to supersede this document or if the FIRST PARTY terminates this agreement for the failure of the SECOND PARTY to comply with any of its provisions. Notice of any failure to comply shall be provided by the FIRST PARTY to the SECOND PARTY immediately upon learning of non-compliance, and the SECOND PARTY shall have 10 days in which to respond and rectify the agreement breach. If a response is not satisfactory or timely made to the FIRST PARTY by the SECOND PARTY, the FIRST PARTY, at the option of the FIRST PARTY, may terminate this agreement.

9. **RIGHT OF INSPECTION:** At any time within reason, the FIRST PARTY may enter on the premises, within reason, for the purpose of viewing the SECOND PARTY'S use of the premises in compliance with this agreement. Once a Notice of Termination of this agreement has been provided to the SECOND PARTY, the FIRST PARTY reserves the right to enter upon the premises for the purpose of farming, planting and harvesting the crops on the premises.

10. **REMEDIES:** If either of the parties violates the terms of this agreement, the other shall have all rights permitted by law to pursue legal and equitable remedies to which the party is entitled. A failure by the SECOND PARTY to pay any rent when due shall be grounds for the termination of this agreement and shall immediately cause all unpaid rent to be due and owing without any additional notice by the FIRST PARTY to the SECOND PARTY. All remedies accorded shall be pursuant to _____ law and shall include Section _____.

11. **SHARECROP:** In the event the parties have agreed that a rental shall be pursuant to a form of share in the crop raised on the premises, all product raised on the premises shall be harvested and located at the specific location to which the parties agree and, in every event, the FIRST PARTY consents. The terms of the sharecrop and the percentage to each party shall be attached hereto as Attachment "A."

12. **LANDLORD LIEN:** The FIRST PARTY shall have a lien on all the SECOND PARTY's personal property located on the above described real estate and shall have a lien on all crops raised on the premises (growing or grown) until such time the payments due for rental by the SECOND PARTY to the FIRST PARTY are made. The SECOND PARTY shall provide a list of the crops grown and sign appropriate financing statements in order to allow

the FIRST PARTY to protect appropriate liens and security interests so that the FIRST PARTY has a first lien and security interest on the crops grown in order to protect the rental due to the FIRST PARTY.

13. **IMPROVEMENTS:** Any buildings, fences or improvements of any kind made by the SECOND PARTY upon the premises during the term of the agreement shall constitute additional rent and shall ensure to the benefit of the real estate and be the property of the FIRST PARTY. No expenses for the improvement of the premises shall be incurred without the expressed permission of the FIRST PARTY except that the SECOND PARTY agrees to maintain, at his cost, all well and other water sewage systems on the premises except in the event of damage caused by natural catastrophe.

14. **GOVERNMENT PROGRAMS:** The participation in any government programs provided by the United States Department of Agriculture for the state of _____ shall be exclusively at the option of the FIRST PARTY. Payments from participation in such programs shall be divided between the FIRST PARTY and the SECOND PARTY as agreed between them in writing. Such agreement shall be attached hereto as Attachment "B."

15. **NOTICES:** All notices contemplated under this lease shall be made in writing, delivered in person or mailed in the United States mail, return receipt requested to the last known address of the recipient.

16. **POSSESSION:** The SECOND PARTY shall receive possession of the premises on the _____ day of _____, 19___ and shall have the premises subject to the terms and conditions of this lease until the _____ day of _____, 19___. In the event of termination of this lease for any reason, the premises shall be relinquished to the possession of the FIRST PARTY.

17. **WRITTEN CHANGES:** Any changes to this agreement must be made in writing and executed by both parties in an addendum to this agreement.

18. **ACCOUNTING:** The method used for dividing and accounting of any harvest of grain, if applicable, shall be performed in the following manner:

19. **APPLICABLE LAW:** The laws of the State of _____ shall apply to this agreement. If either party is compelled to enforce the terms of this agreement, the prevailing party shall be entitled to recover reasonable attorney's fees and costs.

20. **ADDITIONAL PROVISIONS:**

Dated on this _____ day of _____, 19___ at _____, _____.

_____   _____
Owner of Premises/First Party   Leasing Party/Second Party

STATE OF _____   )
)ss
COUNTY OF _____   )

On this _____ day of _____, 19___ before me, the undersigned Notary Public in and for _____ County and the State of _____, personally appeared the individuals who are identified above as the First Party and the Second Party who acknowledged to me to be the persons who are named in the agreement and who executed the foregoing agreement as their voluntary act and deed.

_____
NOTARY PUBLIC

Form Five

PROMISSORY NOTE
(LONG FORM)

DEBTOR: _____

CREDITOR: _____

DATE OF NOTE: _____

AMOUNT OF NOTE: _____

INTEREST RATE: _____

PURPOSE OF NOTE: _____

MATURITY DATE: _____

1. **PROMISE:** ON THIS _____ day of _____, 19___, the undersigned first party (debtor) jointly and severally agree as principals to pay the second party (creditor), its successors, agents and/or assigns the amount of $_____ (principal amount) plus interest in the amount of _____ (rate of interest).

2. **PAYMENT:** The payment of the above noted amount plus interest at the above identified rate shall be paid either: (a) in a single payment in the amount of $_____ (total amount of principal plus total amount of interest) on the maturity date of the _____ day of _____ 19___; or (b) in (number of installments) installments of $_____ on the _____ day of each month after the date of this note until fully paid and, in no event, shall final payment of principal and interest extend beyond the maturity date of this note, the _____ day of _____, 19___. Interest shall be first deducted from the payment made, with the balance of the payment applied to the principal.

3. **INTEREST:** The interest of the principal amount due on this note is _____% per annum. If the interest and principal is not paid when due, the unpaid balance shall draw a higher rate of interest of _____% per annum.

4. **SECURITY:** Any security offered in conjunction with this note is identified as: _____(description of property offered as security). An appropriate UCC form may be filed with the proper authority including the Secretary of State or County Recorder in conjunction with any security interest held in conjunction with this paragraph.

5. **CONSUMER CREDIT:** This agreement is not considered by the parties to be a consumer credit transaction. This transaction is subject to the Uniform Commercial Code of the State of _____.

6. **DEFAULT:** This note shall be considered to be in default whenever there exists: (a) failure to pay either interest or principal when same is due; (b) death of the debtor; (c) failure by the debtor to comply with any provisions of this agreement including the pledging

of items listed as security in this agreement to any other party; (d) insolvency or business failure by the debtor; (e) any assignments for the benefits of other creditors or the filing of bankruptcy by the debtor; (f) any attachments, liens or acquisitions which, in any way, affect property offered in this agreement as security or collateral; (g) any untrue statements, misrepresentations or misstatements made by debtor; or (h) any occurrence of default or breach of any agreements by debtor which may relate to this note or the security offered.

7. **REMEDIES:** In the event of default, all amounts of principal and interest are deemed due and owing to the second party. The second party creditor to this agreement shall be entitled to all remedies permitted by law. Additionally, the second party shall be entitled to recover all expenses related to collection including attorney fees and costs from the first party, if collection is necessary. Such amounts shall be in addition to any interest, penalty interest, and principal amounts due.

8. **LAW APPLICABLE:** The law of the State of _____ shall apply to this agreement. Failure at any time to exercise certain options available to the second party under this control shall not be deemed a waiver of any rights provided under _____ law on this agreement by the second party. The second party may exercise its rights and options under this agreement at a time later than the date when any sums may come due and the second party may make demand for payment at any time after such payments fall due.

9. **INSPECTION:** The second party may inspect, copy and review the first party's books and records at any reasonable time.

10. **ASSIGNMENT OR SALE:** The second party may assign or sell its interest in this agreement at any time and without notice to the first party.

11. **OTHER PROVISIONS:**

Dated at _____ on this _____ day of _____, 19___.

_____
Signature of Second
Party/Creditor

_____
Signature of First
Party/Debtor

_____
Address of Second Party

_____
Address of First Party

This is not a substitute for legal advice. An attorney must be consulted.

Form Six

PROMISSORY NOTE
(SHORT FORM)

The undersigned _____ (debtor or first party) of _____ (first party's address) hereby agrees to pay the sum of $_____ to _____ (creditor or second party) of _____ (second party's address) plus interest from the _____ day of _____, 19___, at the rate of _____% per annum in consideration of: (here state the reason such as money loaned, etc.) Repayment shall be made according to the following schedule:

_____(date) — _____(amount of payment)
_____(date) — _____(amount of payment)
_____(date) — _____(amount of payment)
_____(date) — _____(amount of payment)

Interest due at the time of payment shall be deducted first; then the remainder of the payment shall be applied to principal. Upon failure to pay when due _____ (first party) shall be immediately obligated to pay the full amount of principal, all interest plus costs and attorney fees, if any, incurred for recovery by _____ (second party).

This Note is subject to the laws of the State of _____.

Dated this _____ day of _____, 19___ at _____ (location where note is signed).

_____
Witness Signature

_____
Signature of Debtor/First Party

_____
Address of Debtor/First Party

Form Seven

SECURITY AGREEMENT

Debtor   _____

Address of Debtor   _____

Creditor   _____

Address of Creditor   _____

THIS AGREEMENT, made between the undersigned DEBTOR, _____ of _____ and the undersigned CREDITOR, _____ of _____, is entered in conjunction with the following:

1. **PROPERTY:** The property the undersigned DEBTOR is providing as collateral to the CREDITOR is described as follows:

2. **INDEBTEDNESS:** The debt for which the above noted collateral is offered as security is a result from the debt occurred by the DEBTOR to the CREDITOR as described as follows:

3. **PURPOSE:** The reason for this security interest in the above described property as collateral is to:

4. **DEFAULT:** In the event of default in failure to pay by the DEBTOR to the CREDITOR the amounts due and owing to the CREDITOR pursuant to an agreement evidencing any obligations to the CREDITOR, the result shall be the CREDITOR declaring the obligations immediately due and payable. The CREDITOR shall have all remedies according to a secured party under the Uniform Commercial Code of _____.

5. **FILING:** The CREDITOR (secured party), at his option, may file this security agreement with the Secretary of State or the appropriate County Recorder or both.

6. **ADDITIONAL PROVISIONS:**

_____   _____
DEBTOR   CREDITOR

STATE OF_____   )
)ss
COUNTY OF_____   )

On this _____ day of_____, 19___, the persons identified above, _____ and _____, signed before me, a Notary Public, their signatures when they personally appeared to declare the above voluntary act and deed.

_____
NOTARY PUBLIC

Form Eight

OFFER TO BUY REAL ESTATE

1. **TO:** _____

2. **FROM:** _____

3. **REAL ESTATE:** BUYER hereby offers to purchase real estate in _____ County, _____ from SELLER as described as follows:

4. **SPECIAL ITEMS:** It is understood that the property may be subject to certain easements, zoning requirements, ordinances, restrictive covenants, utility usage, road usage, highway usage, sidewalk usage, etc. This offer is made with the understanding that such special features may be a part of the property. SELLER will provide evidence of any and all special matters through appropriate abstracting upon request.

5. **PURCHASE PRICE:** Purchase price of the aforementioned property shall be $_____ payable by BUYER to SELLER as follows:

6. **TAXES/SPECIAL ASSESSMENTS:** SELLER shall pay all taxes which accrue during the possession of SELLER, and BUYER shall pay all taxes which are accrued subsequent to the possession date set out herein. Any and all special assessments which have accrued during SELLER's possession shall be paid by SELLER. If any special assessments accrue subsequent to the possession date, same shall be paid by BUYER.

7. **INSURANCE:** SELLER shall maintain insurance coverage for liability, fire, theft, casualty, tornado and other property damage until the possession date. After the possession date, the BUYER shall be responsible for all insurance upon the premises.

8. **PROPERTY CONDITION:** The SELLER shall preserve the property in its present condition and have property maintained in such condition until the possession date at which time BUYER will assume possession, maintenance and care of the property. Care and maintenance of the property shall include all fixtures of the property, all trees, shrubs, fences, gates, and interior fixtures such as plumbing, heating, electrical, water heaters, water softeners, air conditioning, blinds, awnings, etc.

9. **POSSESSION:** If this offer is accepted on or before the ____ day of _____, 19___, at _____o'clock __.m. by the SELLER, BUYER shall have possession of the premises on or before the ____ day of _____, 19___. During the period prior to BUYER's possession, SELLER shall maintain the property in its present condition and shall not cause the property to decrease in value or allow for any portion of the property to be damaged or destroyed. SELLER shall preserve all aspects of the property including: the integrity of any and all building exteriors, any and all landscaping, fencing, gates, wells, towers and outbuildings. SELLER shall also maintain all interior integrity of all buildings including: heating systems, plumbing, electrical fixtures, doors, screens, awnings, air conditioning equipment, floor coverings, wall coverings, etc.

10. **DEED/BILL OF SALE:** Once all terms and conditions, including full payment of the consideration for the above described property, have been fulfilled, the SELLER shall execute and deliver a Warranty Deed to the BUYER. The deed shall convey title in fee simple. The SELLER will also demonstrate merchantable title, provide the BUYER with the abstract to the property showing the original government patent and/or platting, title in the SELLER's name and the disclosure of all easements, restrictions and covenants on the property. The SELLER shall pay the abstracting costs to the date of the BUYER's final payment under this contract. A Bill of Sale shall be executed by the SELLER if any personal property is a part of this conveyance. The deed of conveyance may contain restrictions of qualifications as to zoning, easements, restrictive covenants or specific regulatory matters that restrict use of the property. If the property is held in joint tenancy, the deed provided must properly reflect such ownership and conveyance. A spouse not listed on the title shall be presumed to have relinquished all rights of dower, homestead and distributive share.

11. **ENCUMBRANCES:** Any and all encumbrances on the property shall be satisfied by SELLER on or before the date of possession as noted above.

12. **FORFEITURE OF DOWN PAYMENT:** If the BUYER fails to perform under this contract, any payments made may be forfeited to the SELLER at SELLER's option. If SELLER fails to timely perform, the BUYER shall have all payments returned. Both BUYER and SELLER are entitled to utilize any and all other remedies accorded them under the laws of the State of _____ for failure to perform the conditions of this contract.

13. **APPLICABLE LAW:** The law applicable to the enforcement of this contract is the law of the State of _____.

14. **OTHER PROVISIONS:**

Dated at _____ on this _____ day of_____,
19___.

_____   _____
BUYER   SELLER

_____   _____
BUYER   SELLER

STATE OF _____)
)ss
COUNTY OF _____)

On this _____ day of_____, 19___, the persons identified above
(list parties) signed before me, a Notary Public, their signatures when they personally appeared to declare the above voluntary act and deed.

                                                    _____
                                                    NOTARY PUBLIC

This is not a substitute for legal advice. An attorney must be consulted.
Copyright © 1996 by LAW™

Form Nine

REAL ESTATE PURCHASE CONTRACT

THIS AGREEMENT, dated this _____ day of_____, 19___, by and between _____of _____, hereafter referred to as the **Buyer**, and _____ of _____, hereafter referred to as the **Seller**, recites the following terms and conditions:

1. **PROMISE TO PURCHASE REAL ESTATE:** The party of the Seller has agreed to sell certain real estate to the party of the Buyer in conjunction with the consideration, terms and conditions of this agreement. This agreement is subject to the various laws of the State of _____ and may be filed with the appropriate governmental entity in order to provide proper notice to any interested parties and the public.

2. **DESCRIPTION OF PROPERTY:** The property sold by the party of the Seller to the party of the Buyer is legally described as:

The aforementioned property may be subject to various zoning restrictions, easements, restrictive covenants, rules, regulations and laws as a survey of the premises, review of the abstract and the examination of various title documents may demonstrate. The party of the Second Part shall make available to the party of the First Part such documents for review when appropriate or when requested.

3. **CONSIDERATION:** The Buyer shall pay the purchase price of $_____ to the Seller for the above described premises, exclusive of any amounts of interest which may be due by the Buyer to the Seller, pursuant to the following. A down payment of $_____ shall be paid by the Buyer to the Seller on the ____ day of _____, 1996. The balance of the purchase price, $_____, shall be paid by the Buyer to the Seller plus interest at the rate of _____% per month and shall be due on the _____ day of each and every month. The first monthly payment shall be made on the _____ day of _____, 19___ with a payment on the _____ day of every month thereafter until the _____ day of_____, 20___. At the time of the last payment, any remaining and unpaid balance or balloon payment amount shall be made. The balloon amount, providing all regular payments, taxes, special assessments, etc. have been paid by the Buyer, shall be $_____.

4. **<u>TAXES/SPECIAL ASSESSMENT</u>:** The Seller shall pay all taxes and any special assessments which have occurred or been assessed on the property up to and including the _____ day of _____, 19___. The Buyer shall pay all taxes and any special assessments which have accrued or been assessed after the aforementioned date. In conjunction with this provision, the Seller agrees to pay $_____ for any taxes or assessments attributable to his ownership/possession, and the Buyer agrees to pay all other taxes and assessments. If the Buyer fails to pay taxes or assessments when due, the Seller may, to protest interest, pay such amounts. In such event, the Seller may assess the advances plus interest to the Buyer or declare this contract in default in conjunction with the default provision of this contract.

5. **<u>MORTGAGES/ENCUMBRANCES</u>:** The Seller shall, with the proceeds of the payments made by the Buyer, make all payments to other parties who may hold a mortgage or lien in order to satisfy all mortgages and other encumbrances upon the property. The Seller is permitted to make such payments monthly as payments are received from the Buyer. The Buyer shall receive monthly verification from the Seller that the mortgage or other obligations of encumbrances are satisfied to third parties by the Seller. If the Seller fails to provide verification or fails to make the required mortgage or encumbrance payment obligations, the Buyer may make arrangements for the monthly obligation to the Seller under this contract to be paid directly to the party who holds a mortgage or other encumbrance on the property. Once the Buyer has reduced the balance of this contract to the existing mortgage or encumbrance amounts, the Buyer may, if permitted by the party holding the mortgage or encumbrance, either assume the mortgage or encumbrance or pay the monthly amounts directly to the holder of the mortgage or encumbrance. Such payments would occur in the event the Seller's equity interest has been paid to the Seller .

6. **<u>INSURANCE</u>:** The Buyer, from the date of possession forward, shall maintain insurance coverage for all liability, fire, tornado, flooding, other hazards and contingencies as the Seller may require on all buildings existing or erected on the above described premises and the contents, if any of the contents have also been sold by the Seller to the Buyer. The Buyer shall obtain an appropriate rider on the insurance policies, with the Seller identified as the owner in fee simple of the premises. In the event of any loss, the Seller must be a co-payee of insurance proceeds in order to assure the proper replacement or repair or loss to the premises.

7. **NEW ENCUMBRANCES/LIENS:** Neither party may encumber the above described property in any way during the term of this agreement unless specific written consent is received by the other party.

8. **DEED/BILL OF SALE:** Once all terms and conditions, including full payment of the consideration for the above described property, have been fulfilled, the Seller shall execute and deliver a Warranty Deed to the Buyer. The deed shall convey title in fee simple. TIhe Seller will also demonstrate merchantable title, provide the Buyer with the abstract to the property showing the original government patent and/or platting, title in the Seller's name and the disclosure of all easements, restrictions and covenants on the property. The Seller shall pay the abstracting costs to the date of the Buyer's final payment under this contract. A Bill of Sale shall be executed by the Seller if any personal property is a part of this conveyance. The deed of conveyance may contain restrictions or qualifications as to zoning, easements, restrictive covenants or specific regulatory matters that restrict use of the property. If the property is held in joint tenancy, the deed provided must properly reflect such ownership and conveyance.

9. **FORFEITURE/FORECLOSURE:** If the Buyer fails to perform any portion of this contract, as agreed, the Seller may take appropriate action to reclaim the property including the legal action of contract forfeiture. In the event forfeiture is necessary, the Seller shall also be entitled to attorney fees and costs. The failure of any of the following may constitute grounds for forfeiture: (a) payment of amounts due under this contract; (b) payment of taxes and/or special assessments; (c) maintaining insurance; (d) maintaining the premises in good condition and/or reasonable repair; (e) using the premises for lawful purposes; (f) complying with applicable law regarding use of the premises and; (g) complying with the provision of this contract. Additionally, the failure to comply with the provision of this agreement by the Buyer, shall give the Seller the right to issue a _____ day notice to accelerate the payment of the entire balance of this contract.

10. **INTEREST ON DELINQUENCY:** On any amounts deemed to be delinquent by either party under this contract, _____% interest per annum may be applied on such delinquent amounts.

11. **POSSESSION:** The Buyer shall take possession of the premises on the _____ day of _____, 19___.

12. **APPLICABLE LAW:** The laws of the State of _____ shall govern the terms and conditions of this contract.

13. **OTHER PROVISIONS:**

Dated at _____ this ____ day of _____, 19___.

_____   _____

_____   _____

_____   _____

Name and Address of Seller   Name and Address of Buyer

_____   _____

_____   _____

Name and Address of Spouse   Name and Address of Spouse

STATE OF_____)

)

COUNTY OF _____)

On this ____ day of_____, 19___, the persons identified above, _____,_____, signed before me, a Notary Public, their signatures when they personally appeared to declare the above voluntary act and deed.

_____

NOTARY PUBLIC

Form Ten

BILL OF SALE

THIS AGREEMENT between _____ of _____, hereinafter SELLER, and _____ of _____, hereinafter BUYER, is for the sale of the following:

1. **PROPERTY AS IS:** The property as described above is sold by the SELLER to the BUYER as the property is seen and observed with any and all faults which it may have.

2. **PURCHASE PRICE:** The BUYER agrees to pay to the SELLER, at SELLER's address, the amount of $_____. Payment shall be made by the BUYER to the SELLER in the following manner:

3. **DEFAULT:** In the event BUYER fails to make payment or is otherwise in default in paying the SELLER, the SELLER has all rights to reclaim the property and/or the SELLER may declare the entire balance due, if any sums are left unpaid.

4. **INTEREST RATE:** The interest rate for any unpaid sums shall be the rate of _____% per annum.

5. **DELIVERY OF PROPERTY:** In the event of default, at the demand of SELLER, the BUYER must deliver the goods to the SELLER at the address listed above and in the same condition in which BUYER acquired the property from SELLER.

Dated this _____ day of _____, 19___, at _____.

_____   _____
BUYER   SELLER

STATE OF_____)
)ss
COUNTY OF_____)

On this _____ day of_____, 19___, the persons identified above, _____, _____, signed before me, a Notary Public, their signatures when they personally appeared to declare the above voluntary act and deed.

_____
NOTARY PUBLIC

Form Eleven

SUBCONTRACTOR PERFORMANCE AGREEMENT FOR RESIDENTIAL CONSTRUCTION

_____

THIS AGREEMENT, entered this _____ day of _____, 19___, between _____ of _____ and _____ of _____ is established and conditioned on the following terms:

1. **PARTY STATUS:** Owner shall serve as the general contractor on the building project described in paragraph two herein. Subcontractor shall serve in his own capacity as a legal entity known as an Independent Contractor and, accordingly, shall employ, compensate and manage any assistance required for performance of this contract. Subcontractor shall be responsible for: liability insurance for work related to this project, workers' compensation for its employees, appropriate tax withholding (federal, state and local), appropriate job service taxes (federal, state and local), and all union relations. Subcontractor shall hold owner/builder harmless and thereby indemnify owner/builder for any claims made which may be generated from work related to this project.

2. **JOB SITE:** The job site for this project shall be kept free of debris, trash, dangerous conditions, and potential hazards by subcontractor, and said subcontractor shall leave the following described premises in a clean and injury-free environment at the conclusion of each work day. The job site premises is described as follows:

3. **COMPLIANCE STANDARDS:** Subcontractor shall comply with all federal, state and local laws, rules and regulations including, but not limited to, OSHA standards. Subcontractor shall hold owner/builder harmless for any violations and shall, accordingly, indemnify said owner/builder.

4. **TERM:** The term of this agreement is for the construction period required for the construction of the aforementioned project (described in paragraph 2). Limitation and deadlines on said project are as follows:

a) 50% of the "rough in" work to be performed by subcontractor shall be completed by the _____ day of _____, 19___.

b) An additional 30% of the total amount of the work to be performed by subcontractor shall be completed by the _____ day of _____, 19___.

c) The final 20% of the total work to be performed by subcontractor shall be completed by the _____ day of _____, 19___.

d) In the event the work to be performed as set forth above is not completed as stated, the liquidated damages provision of this agreement shall apply.

5. **LIQUIDATED DAMAGES:** In the event subcontractor fails to perform in conjunction with the workmanship provision (paragraph 7) or any other provision of this agreement or if there is a failure to meet the deadlines set out in paragraph 4 (or as modified in paragraph 6 herein), subcontractor shall be penalized the sum of $_____ per day.

6. **WEATHER DAYS:** Only in the event the parties agree in writing to extensions for bad weather days will exceptions be allowed for the deadlines of paragraph 4 or the liquidated damages of paragraph 5 above. Weather day extensions will not be unreasonably withheld by owner/contractor; however, such extensions must be for good cause shown since the parties in this agreement contemplate that 15 bad weather days have already been included in the deadlines set forth in paragraph 4 above.

7. **WORKMANSHIP:** Subcontractor agrees to provide lasting and quality work for the items set forth in the attached "estimate " or "quote" for services. Said work will be subject to the approval of owner/builder prior to payment for said services. Subcontractor warrants his work and will make or pay for any and all repairs or corrections which are necessary due to faulty or improper craftsmanship.

8. **MATERIALS:** Subcontractor shall provide all quality material necessary for the work on the project (premises) described in paragraph two above subject to the following:

9. **PAYMENT:** Owner/builder will pay to subcontractor the total sum of $_____ as set forth in the attached "estimate" or "quote" and no more, unless a change order is made and signed by the parties for any items not included in the attached "estimate" or "quote." Without a change order duly executed, any additional items will be provided by subcontractor at subcontractor's expense. Payment shall be made by owner/contractor to subcontractor on the following basis:

		PERCENTAGE
AMOUNT	**DATE**	**OF COMPLETION**

a)

b)

c)

10. **EMPLOYEES:** Subcontractor may, at his discretion, hire additional help to assist on the aforementioned project; however, any such assistance will be paid by subcontractor. Payment for additional help shall be the sole obligation of subcontractor, and such payment shall include, but is not limited to: all taxes, withholding, job service, workers' compensation and any other governmental obligations, as well as, salaries which subcontractor is required to pay.

11. **INSURANCE:** Subcontractor shall maintain all appropriate forms of insurance including, but not limited to: workers' compensation, health and accident, general liability and any other form of insurance requested by owner/builder. Owner/builder shall be listed as a protected party under such policies of insurance. Subcontractor shall hold owner/builder harmless for any accident which may occur "on" or "to and from" the job site which, in any way, relates to subcontractor's work on the aforementioned project. Proof of insurance coverage shall be provided to owner/builder within 20 days after the signing of this agreement. Commencement of this project will not occur until subcontractor has provided proof of insured coverage.

12. **RIGHT TO INSPECT:** Owner/builder shall have the right to inspect the project at all times and the additional right to stop the project and terminate this agreement if subcontractor's work is not done in a workmanlike and quality manner acceptable to owner/builder.

13. **LIEN WAIVERS:** The contractor shall provide to the owner appropriate lien waivers upon receipt of payment as set forth in paragraph 9 above.

14. **<u>ADDITIONAL PROVISIONS:</u>**

a)

b)

c)

Dated this _____ day of _____, 19___.

_____

SUBCONTRACTOR

_____

OWNER/BUILDER

_____

WITNESS

_____

WITNESS

Form Twelve

DEADLINE EXTENSION AMENDMENT

The parties in authority as identified below hereby agree to amend the subcontractor performance agreement for residential construction:

a) 15 Bad Weather Days which are identified in paragraph 6 of the subcontractor performance agreement which have already occurred are:

Day of Week	Date	Owner/Contractor Initials	Subcontractor Initials

1.
2.
3.
4.
5.
6.
7.
8.
9.
10.
11.
12.
13.
14.
15.

b) The total of _____ additional days will be permitted as an extension to the deadlines set forth in paragraph 4 of the subcontractor performance agreement before liquidated damages (paragraph 5 of said contract) are imposed.

Dated at _____ on this _____ day of _____, 19___.

_____   _____
Owner/Contractor   Subcontractor

This is not a substitute for legal advice. An attorney must be consulted.

Form Thirteen

WAIVER OF LIEN

The undersigned contractor of _____, _____, does hereby provide the following waiver of any and all liens on the construction project at _____ in _____, _____, to _____, the (owner/contractor):

1. The parties have previously entered into a construction project for labor and/or materials as shown on the attached estimate and/or attached description;

2. The attached documents contain a description of any and all work that was to be performed at the aforementioned project;

3. The work has been performed and the materials provided in conjunction with the complete agreement(s);

4. In consideration of _____ Dollars ($_____) receipt of which is hereby acknowledged as payment in _____(full/part), the undersigned contractor waives all claims of lien and right of lien that he may obtain against such property by having performed the services described on the attached.

IN WITNESS WHEREOF, the undersigned contractor executes this waiver and release on this _____ day of _____, 19___.

_____   _____
WITNESS   CONTRACTOR

This is not a substitute for legal advice. An attorney must be consulted.

Index